MW01193992

The Theology of the
Levitical Priesthood

The Theology of the Levitical Priesthood

Assisting God's People in Their Mission
to the Nations

NICHOLAS HAYDOCK

WIPF & STOCK · Eugene, Oregon

THE THEOLOGY OF THE LEVITICAL PRIESTHOOD
Assisting God's People in Their Mission to the Nations

Copyright © 2015 Nicholas Haydock. All rights reserved. Except for brief quotations in critical publications or reviews, no part of this book may be reproduced in any manner without prior written permission from the publisher. Write: Permissions, Wipf and Stock Publishers, 199 W. 8th Ave., Suite 3, Eugene, OR 97401.

Wipf & Stock
An Imprint of Wipf and Stock Publishers
199 W. 8th Ave., Suite 3
Eugene, OR 97401

www.wipfandstock.com

ISBN 13: 978-1-62564-743-6
Manufactured in the U.S.A.

Scripture taken from the New American Standard Bible®, © Copyright 1960, 1962, 1963, 1968, 1971, 1972, 1973, 1975, 1977, 1995 by The Lockman Foundation. Used by permission.

For my parents

Contents

Acknowledgments

I GRATEFULLY ACKNOWLEDGE THOSE who have supported me in this writing project. Beginning with the encouragement shown to me from the very start, through my siblings in Christ, Ben and Helen Care. I am also indebted both to my wise friend Anna Bishop and to Dr. Nobuyoshi Kiuchi, for their feedback and comments which assisted me in preparing the manuscript for publication.

As this manuscript started its life as a piece of study conducted at Redcliffe College, Gloucestershire; I would also like to acknowledge the guidance I received from Dr. Tim Davy in particular.

Introduction

THE LEVITICAL PRIESTHOOD[1] HAD a central role in Israel's cultic life, and has become one of the most disputed areas of modern scholarship.[2] What then can be achieved in such a short study, which neither attempts to divulge the complexities of modern critical scholarship, nor to examine every reference to the Levites in the biblical corpus?

This thematic study seeks to expose the theology of the Levitical priesthood, for the benefit of the church. It is a canonical reading of the priesthood which directly challenges many of the assumptions and findings of critical scholarship, and in so doing resources the church to faithfully reflect on her participation within God's mission. The central hypothesis of this project is that the priesthood's service was to be made acceptable through suffering humility; this would enable the whole nation of Israel to participate in God's mission to the nations.

In setting the scene for this study, the introduction will look at the role that the priesthood has played in biblical theology and missiological reflection, respectively.

---

1. To be clear from the beginning, by using the phrase "Levitical priesthood," the study is not isolating itself to the so called "deuteronomistic" conception of priesthood, where there is supposedly no distinction between priest and Levite. For a detailed refutation of this view, consult Gordon McConville (*Law and Theology in Deuteronomy*). Rather, here it is held that there is a coherent theology of the priesthood which spans the whole canon.

2. Vangemeren, *New International Dictionary*, 1066.

THE ROLE OF THE PRIESTHOOD IN BIBLICAL THEOLOGY

Despite the central role which the priesthood played in Israel's life and worship, the majority of Old Testament theologies neglect to explore the peculiarities of Israel's priesthood; perhaps a result of Protestantism's aversion to the cult.[3]

Biblical theology, influenced by Wellhausen's reconstruction of Israel's history, came to see the Levitical priesthood as a postexilic innovation, the fruit of a struggle within the priesthood for power at the time of the exile. As such, material relating to the priests was treated as legalistic and religiously inferior.[4] Wellhausen understood the demarcation between Aaronic and Levitical priests to be a late construction and for many years this view was the only accepted approach to understanding Israel's cultic life.[5] This is not to suggest however, that others did not seek to modify Wellhausen's theory,[6] nor that those who attempted to reconstruct the history of Israelites ever achieved a consensus of opinion. One of the issues which divide scholars who hold to such reconstructed histories is the extent to which earlier practices are represented in the biblical accounts, or indeed if they can be said to represent them at all.[7] Some thinkers, such as Curtiss and Gunneweg,[8] for example, challenged the dating of a postexilic construction, but their reconstructions, though less radical than Wellhausen's, were nonetheless still reconstructions which differed from the "biblical presentation."[9]

---

3. Brueggemann, *Theology of the Old Testament*, 652.

4. Brueggemann, *Theology of the Old Testament*, 653.

5. Von Rad, *Old Testament Theology*, 249.

6. One notable modification, was that put forward by Frank Cross (*Canaanite Myth and Hebrew Epic*, 197), who proposed that the struggle was not so much between Levitical and Aaronic priesthoods, but rather between Moses' and Aaron's priesthood.

7. Cross, *Canaanite Myth and Hebrew Epic*, 198.

8. Curtiss, *Levitical Priests*; Gunneweg, *Understanding the Old Testament*.

9. Childs, *Old Testament Theology in a Canonical Context*, 147.

Both linguistically and conceptually, these historical reconstructions have been shown to be false. Linguistically, research has pointed to the chronological priority of "P," the parts of the Scripture supposedly added by priestly editors, over Ezekiel.[10] Conceptually, developments within the Levites' practice aren't reflected back. So for example it has been noted that the Levitical practices of using utensils in 1 Chronicles 9:28–32 is different to the hands-off approach in Numbers 4:4–14,[11] and that in Ezekiel the Levites are given the task of slaying the burnt offering, which in Leviticus is reserved for the laity.[12]

Moreover attempts at reconstructing Israel's history assumed a progressive evolution in the religious institutions from the simple to the complex, which is foreign to the biblical evidence.

The publication of Childs's *Old Testament Theology in a Canonical Context* marked an important turning point in Old Testament theology. Childs argued that the basis of our theological reflection is not the events behind the text, but rather the text itself, and for that reason he moved for a canonical approach to Scripture.[13] Childs rightly perceived that by reordering the text diachronically, Scripture's message had been missed.[14] A canonical approach requires that Israel's history is read as a corruption of God's intention as the text intimates, not as an innovation.[15]

By adopting Childs's canonical approach, the reader is liberated from merely searching the text for hidden political forces.[16] This will be an essential component for this study, because as already stated, it is believed that the key to understanding the

10. Block, *Book of Ezekiel*, 635.

11. Ashley, *Book of Numbers*, 91.

12. These differences, which can partly be explained by the erection of the temple (Wenham, *Numbers*, 86), show that the shape of the priesthood altered throughout history, and that these changes are accurately recorded in the biblical accounts.

13. Childs, *Old Testament*, 6.

14. Ibid., 153.

15. Ibid., 152.

16. Ibid., 148.

Levites' role is to see them as a body which must serve with humility before God and his people, not a political force with their own self-centered agenda. Such a reading is fundamentally in opposition to the aforementioned reconstructed histories, which assume that the priesthood who had acquired power sought to provide divine justification for their superiority.

Even still, the canonical approach has had its critics. Brueggemann, while placing great value in Childs's work, criticizes it for being in his opinion "massively reductionistic"; he argues that to limit the reading of the Old Testament to what is useful for Christian theology, is to disregard much of the text.[17] In Childs's defense though, he clearly states that the Old Testament is not just a foil for the New.[18]

It has also been argued that all the canonical approach really amounts to is a return to pre-critical exegesis.[19] As has been argued by others elsewhere though; while aspects of pre-critical exegesis which muted the text must be avoided, it would be wrong to view the historical critical method as a type of "hermeneutical savior," for it also has in its way muted the voice of the text.[20]

It is hoped that further refutation for these objections will be evidenced in this study itself; in the manner of handling Old Testament texts and in the way that the Old Testament witness is given a voice to speak equal to that of the New Testament, most notably in the last chapter which looks at the priesthood and the New Covenant.

Before moving on from this section, it is worth noting which functions have traditionally been ascribed to the priesthood from within biblical theology. The theological intentions of Israel's cultic life have often been overlooked by critical scholarship, which was more interested in speculating as to the political motivation behind the text.[21] At other times the theological implications of

---

17. Brueggemann, *Theology of the Old Testament*, 92.

18. Childs, *Old Testament Theology*, 17.

19. Barton, *Reading the Old Testament*, 84.

20. Blackburn, *God Who Makes Himself Known*, 21.

21. Brueggemann, *Theology of the Old Testament*, 653.

Israel's worship were interpreted through the framework of historical reconstructions, which reduced the priesthood's original role to that of a consultant.[22] Nonetheless most of the priesthood's key responsibilities have not been completely unnoticed. The priests were to bless the people, make legal proclamations, teach, offer sacrifices, discern God's will and care for the sanctuary. All of these functions will be noted during the course of this study, and indeed other functions shall be drawn out as well, for instance looking at the priesthood as a gift and a sacrifice. This study also goes deeper than traditional understandings of the priesthood in that most Old Testament theologies speak of the priests representing God to the people and the people before God,[23] but as shall be explained, the priests also represent the people to the people, providing them with an image of what the nation should look like.

THE PRIESTHOOD IN BIBLE AND MISSION LITERATURE

Childs called for biblical theology to revisit the Levitical priesthood from a canonical perspective,[24] a challenge which has by and large been ignored. The conviction expressed in this study's hypothesis, though, is that it is not only a canonical reading of the Levitical priesthood which is needed, but one which is also missional. In truth, a missional reading of the text has to be canonical by definition, because it requires the canon to be read through the lens of God's mission to the world.[25]

A missional reading can only be valid if it recognizes the cost involved in participating in God's mission. Chris Wright has recently written observing the "missional cost" of participating in God's story with regard to prophethood;[26] a sentiment echoed by

22. Barton and Bowden, *Original Story*, 172.

23. Routledge, *Old Testament Theology*, 184.

24. Childs, *Old Testament Theology*, 150.

25. Beeby, *Canon and Mission*, 39.

26. Wright, "Prophet to the Nations."

others also, for example Goheen and Blackburn.[27] The costliness of mission is important, partly because humility is a prerequisite to participation, but also because God must humble Himself in order for revelation to take place. For the Christian this is no surprise given Christ's death, yet this truth is also seen in the Old Testament and the Levitical priesthood is just one example of this.

Traditionally, Bible and mission literature has given little consideration to the priesthood. The early work done by Lapham neglected to mention the Levites,[28] a trend which was to be followed by other missiologists such as Rowley and Kane.[29] Martin-Achard and Blauw were among the first to argue that Exodus 19:6, "you shall be to Me a kingdom of priests and a holy nation," has a pivotal role in understanding the mission of God in the Old Testament.[30] However, they were mainly interested in emphasizing the universalistic aspects of Israel's mission, and failed to mention the missional function of the priesthood itself. This trend was also mimicked by others such as Peters, Kaiser, Bauckham, Okoye, and Goheen.[31]

In recent times Chris Wright has highlighted the role of the priest in teaching the law and offering sacrifices, allowing this to inform his reading of Exodus 19:6 and consequently his understanding of Israel's mission to the nations.[32] He argued that just as

27. Goheen, *Light to the Nation*, 38; Blackburn, *God Who Makes Himself Known*, 211.

28. Lapham, *Bible as Missionary Handbook*.

29. Rowley, *Missionary Message of the Old Testament*; Kane and Lindsell, *Christian Missions in Biblical Perspective*.

30. Martin-Achard, *Light to the Nations*; Blauw, *Missionary Nature of the Church*, 26.

31. Peters, *Biblical Theology of Missions*, 113; Kaiser, *Mission in the Old Testament*; Bauckham, *Bible and Mission*, 36; Okoye, *Israel and the Nations*; Goheen, *Light to the Nations*, 39. Goheen further makes reference to Exod 19:6 in making the point that mission in the Old Testament is "centripetal"; calling the nations to come to Israel, rather than "centrifugal," going out into the nations. However Exod 19:6 cannot be used to substantiate such an argument however, for it could be argued that just as the Levites were spread throughout the land, so Israel was to go into all nations.

32. Wright, *Mission of God*, 330.

the priests taught the law to Israel, so Israel was to teach the law to the nations and just as the priests led Israelites into worship so the nation were to do for the Gentiles.

Ross Blackburn has similarly focused on the priest's representation of the Lord to Israel, and the representation of Israel before the Lord, within the context of Israel's missionary purpose, with specific reference to the book of Exodus.[33] While these findings have underpinned the approach taken here, it is clear that more could be said, considering that the priesthood did more than just teach and offer sacrifices.

The following chapters will in turn consider particular functions and metaphors associated with the priesthood; paying attention to their costly and missional dimensions, where appropriate. The exceptions to this will be the first and final chapters. The first chapter, "Locating the Priesthood within the Community," will provide the basis for much of this study by considering the priesthood from a sociological perspective. This will be imperative for understanding how the priesthood were to function in the midst of a broader missional community. Meanwhile the last chapter puts forward the case for reading the Levites' ongoing relevance in Christ.

33. Blackburn, *God Who Makes Himself Known*, 91.

1

Locating the Priesthood within the Community

THIS CHAPTER WILL ANALYZE the Levitical priesthood from a sociological perspective. In so doing the particular relationship between the Levites and the rest of Israelite society will be highlighted.

BIBLICAL THEOLOGY AND THE USE OF SOCIAL SCIENCES

The application of the social sciences in biblical studies, is a much discussed issue and fraught with disagreement. To begin with, sociologists have been reluctant to apply sociological theories to historical evidence because it is difficult to test the veracity of the theory itself.[1] This should be readily acknowledged, for it would be unsound for a theologian to implement a sociological theorem which had not been sufficiently tested. As well as this though, Richard Coggins has questioned the use of "fossilized evidence" in sociological study which was not intended to present

1. Rodd, "On Applying Sociological Theory," 33.

a reconstruction of Israelite society.[2] To give attention to both of these objections requires recognition that the Bible is not an ancient sociological record, though this need not entail a denial of the historical reliability of Scripture.

While remaining aware of the objections noted above, this research on the Levitical priesthood will make use of contemporary sociology, drawing upon the work of Mary Douglas in particular. The purpose here is not to reconstruct Israelite society from a particular moment in their history, but rather to consider the ideological presentation of Israelite society, which is carried throughout the canon. As such, the apprehensions of some sociologists are not directly applicable, mainly because this is a theological study making use of sociological theory, not a sociological study making use of the Bible. Indeed, by approaching this subject primarily from the discipline of biblical theology, the option has not been given, whether or not to employ sociological theory. It is impossible for biblical theology to ignore the social dimensions of Israelite society, because literature is itself a social expression.[3]

The focus on sociology will inform this study in a couple of ways. First, as will be argued, the structure of Israelite society itself was to embody God's holiness and love. As a result, even the structure of God's society is missional: revealing the God they serve. In addition to this, sociological study will also enable understanding of the distinctiveness of the Levitical priesthood, in comparison to those belonging to other nations.

GRID AND GROUP THEORY

Mary Douglas first developed the "grid and group" model in 1970, in an effort to provide anthropologists with a tool to aid them in cultural comparison.[4] Being heavily influenced by the work of Durkheim, who argued that there was a correlation between

---

2. Coggins, *Introducing the Old Testament*, 63.

3. Gottwald, *Hebrew Bible*, 31.

4. Douglas, *Natural Symbols*, 3.

a society's structure and their understanding of God,[5] Douglas attempted to relate different belief systems to different types of society. Over a period of many years, Douglas developed the "grid and group" model, and adapted it for a variety of uses in different aspects of her work.[6] The diagram below is the one used in her study of Israelite society presented in the book of Numbers.[7]

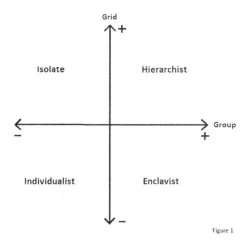

Figure 1

In this model "grid" refers to the structure of a culture; those with a high grid, namely isolate and hierarchist societies, emphasize position and exhibit varying levels of status and power. Conversely those with a low grid, individualist and enclavist societies, display inclinations toward the equality of each member in society regardless of their position and influence. On the horizontal axis, the term "group" relates to the sense of community. In cultures which exhibit high group, the hierarchist and enclavist societies, the community exerts a high degree of pressure on the individual. Whereas in low group societies, isolate and individualist cultures, the individual is not bound in the same way to the group but rather

5. Durkheim, and Swain, *Elementary Forms of the Religious Life*.

6. Douglas, "Background of the Grid Dimension," 171.

7. Douglas, *In the Wilderness*, 45.

has the freedom to influence the rest of society and redefine cultural norms.

It has been suggested that the "grid and group" oversimplifies the complex nature of society.[8] Consequently both Isenberg and Gross have made separate attempts to identify "predicates" from which one might better discern the grid and group of any given society.[9] So while other sociologists have developed the model, its overall worth has not been negated but has rather been hugely influential in contemporary sociological theory.[10]

It might otherwise be suggested that Durkheim's hypothesis on the relationship between a society and God is either wrong or limited in scope. For the purpose of researching the role of the priesthood, however, a Durkheimian approach to religion in society is certainly viable, since Israel was to be holy in imitation of their God (Lev 20:26). God was to be embodied in Israelite society and Israelite society was to be a reflection of their God, such that both communally and individually, the Israelites would represent the God they served to the surrounding nations. For these reasons it seems well to maintain Douglas's application of the model to the book of Numbers.

In her research, Douglas argues that Israel as a whole was an enclavist society, within which the priesthood functioned as a minority hierarchist group.[11] The only irregularity to this suggestion is that typically in an enclavist society the membership boundaries are more restrictive, for in Israel, it is not contact with a foreigner which is defiling, only idolatry.[12] Although Douglas limited her study to the book of Numbers, Ramirez's employment of the model to Amos,[13] Johnson's work on Hebrews[14] and White's study

---

8. Steinfels, "Myth of Primitive Religion," 50.

9. Isenberg and Owen, "Bodies Natural and Contrived"; Gross, *Measuring Culture*.

10. Johnson, *Going Outside the Camp*, 22.

11. Douglas, *In the Wilderness*, 49.

12. Ibid.

13. Ramirez, "Social Location," 124.

14. Johnson, *Going Outside the Camp*.

on the Sermon on the Mount,[15] also reckon that the ideological culture of God's people was that of the enclavist.

Given the supposition that the priesthood function as a hierarchist group within an enclavist society, it is of particular interest for this study to note the differences between these two categories, and consider how they coexist. Therefore the key differences between them will be first identified, and then further reflection on the implications for Israelite society will be given.

Typically in enclavist societies, leaders are to be very humble, as Moses was (Num 12:3).[16] In enclave politics therefore, it is necessary for those in positions of authority to make a show of their weakness and so for instance, it makes perfect sense to Douglas that the Levites receive no inheritance in the promised land.[17] Another difference between enclavist and hierarchist cultures, are the attributes they most readily identify with God. A hierarchist society empathizes with God as a God of justice, where an enclavist group will more readily attend to a compassionate God.[18] Somewhat related to this is the difference in religious practice; hierarchist groups tend to be more concerned with the outward form of religious practice, whereas in enclavist groups a pure heart is more important.[19]

That the Levites function as a minority hierarchist group in the midst of an enclavist society is of great significance for researching the relationship between the priesthood and the rest of Israel. With regard to the point that hierarchist societies are more concerned with outward forms of worship, it seems likely that the Levitical priesthood were meant to be an outward symbol of an inner reality grasped by the whole of Israel. This point will be further evidenced upon looking at the concept of Israel being a "royal priesthood" below. At this point though, it should be affirmed that outward symbols are not bad in and of themselves, but only when

15. White, "Grid and Group," 87.

16. Douglas, *In the Wilderness*, 58.

17. Ibid., 59.

18. Ibid., 56.

19. Ibid., 56.

they become void of their true meaning. Similarly it would be wrong to dualize between pious intentions and outward expressions of faith; it is not true that the priests needed only to perform the ritual meticulously even if they did it with the wrong attitude.[20]

An additional difference between the two societies is the attributes they most readily identify with God. The structure of Israelite society indicates that their God is both compassionate and just; that the priesthood function as a minority within an enclavist society suggests that God's justice needs to be framed by his compassion. The priesthood remind the people that God is just and cannot tolerate sin, yet this needs to be understood in the context of his loving kindness, which is exhibited by the wider social structure of Israel.

One last point to draw from this analysis has to do with leadership. As already put forward, an enclavist society requires leaders who are able to demonstrate humility. This point is exemplified in the story of Korah's rebellion (Num 16). A group headed by Korah, a Levite, rises up in opposition to the leadership of Moses and Aaron. In response Moses asserts that the whole of Israel is holy, so they have no reason to exalt themselves above anyone else (Num 16:3). The priesthood as a body which has responsibility and power must choose to suffer humility for the benefit of others, and thereby become representative of the God they serve.

God is enmeshed within Israel's social framework;[21] he is a God of power who humbly presents himself in weakness for the benefit of others, a point which will be further reinforced throughout this study. The main focus in this section has been on the relationship between Israel's social structure and the God they serve.

---

20. An illustration of this might be seen in Lev 10; Nadab and Abihu brought fire before the Lord, though God had not commanded them to do this (10:1) and the result was that they died for this transgression. Yet later in the same chapter, Aaron, Eleazar and Ithamar, burn up the whole of the sin offering instead of eating their share (10:16). Initially Moses is angry that they have disobeyed God, but when he realized that the fear of the Lord influenced their behavior he approved of their actions.

21. Brueggemann, "Theodicy in a Social Dimension," 263.

In the next section, attention is given to consider further the relationship between the priesthood and the whole nation of Israel.

A KINGDOM OF PRIESTS

> "Now then, if you will indeed obey My voice and keep
> My covenant, then you shall be My own possession
> among all the peoples, for all the earth is Mine; and you
> shall be to Me a kingdom of priests and a holy nation."
> These are the words that you shall speak to the sons of
> Israel. (Exod 19:5–6)

As previously postulated, the priesthood were to be an outward sign of Israel's spiritual reality. This is a key point and one which comes to the fore in Exodus 19:6, a verse which helps to determine the relationship between the Levites and the rest of Israel. These verses act as a "hinge" in the book of Exodus, coming between the story of the Exodus (Exod 1–18) and the giving of the law (Exod 20–24), and so define God's purpose for them as a people.[22] The nation was to be a "kingdom of priests,"[23] and in the same way that the priests were to be a blessing to the Israelites, so the whole nation were to be a blessing to the nations around them, in order that they too might come to worship God.[24]

There has been some discussion among scholars as to what aspects of the priesthood are being imparted to the nation as a whole. It has been variously argued, that the phrase conveys the

---

22. Wright, *Mission of God*, 330.

23. The precise meaning of this phrase is widely discussed and the grammar allows for a variety of interpretations; it could mean "a kingdom consisting of priests," "a priestly kingdom," "a royal priesthood," "a kingdom under the authority of priests," or "a kingdom which rules over a people of priests" (Wells, *God's Holy People*). Given the wider context though it is best understood as "priestly kingdom," for we see elsewhere that the priesthood are representative of the whole nation; for instance the twelve stones which are worn on Aaron's breastplate.

24. McNeile, *Book of Exodus*, 111.

concept that Israel should worship God alone,[25] that they should demonstrate holiness in their way of life[26] and that all Israelites had direct access to God.[27] Nonetheless there is no reason to suggest that this metaphor conveys only one aspect of the priesthood's function. Instead it seems better to understand that the metaphor divulges the dialectical relationship between the priesthood and Israel as a whole; informing Israel's relationships with the surrounding nations, in numerous ways.[28]

Cornelis Houtman contends with those who read Exodus 19:4–6 missionally, arguing that neither Exodus 19:4–6 nor its immediate context, state that Israel has a missional purpose to the surrounding nations.[29] However this simply ignores the fact that the preceding chapters tell the story of how God revealed himself to Pharaoh and the Egyptian people. In fact it has been elsewhere argued that the central theme of the book of Exodus is that God wants to make himself known to the nations.[30]

The universalistic dimension of the priesthood's ministry is seen also at other places in Scripture, for example Ezekiel 47. Ezekiel, ministering during the time of Israel's exile, assures Israel that God has not abandoned them despite their disobedience and the destruction of the temple; he will continue to be faithful to them and dwell amongst them. Ezekiel 47 contains a vision of something new that God will do, yet very much in continuation with what his intentions and purposes for Israel have always been. Ezekiel saw rivers flowing out in all directions emanating from the temple and giving life to all Israel and the world; thereby demonstrating that God's presence will be mediated through the priesthood and a restored Israel to bless the nations.[31]

25. Langston, *Exodus through the Centuries*, 219.

26. Ashby, *Go Out and Meet God*, 87.

27. Hyatt, *Commentary on Exodus*, 200.

28. Fretheim, *Exodus*, 212.

29. Houtman, *Exodus*, 446.

30. Blackburn, *God Who Makes Himself Known*.

31. Allen, *Ezekiel 20–48*, 285.

The Levitical priesthood were meant to be the ultimate model of holiness to the Israelite. They were to be a visible example to the rest of Israel of what it meant to serve God, and in turn Israel as a whole was to be a showcase to the world of what being in relationship with God looked like.[32] This relationship impacted the political, social and economic dimensions of Israel's life and witness. Scholars who believe that Israel's priesthood was intended to resemble those of the surrounding nations, miss the point here; that Israel was to be a "kingdom of priests" does not mean that they were to assume a more elevated position above the nations, rather it means they were to be "servant nation."[33] The findings in this section directly challenge attitudes which are often held by biblical theologians toward the priesthood, outlined in the introduction; the Levites must take on a lowly position in order to serve both God and his people.

32. Durham, *Exodus*, 263.
33. Ibid.

2

The Priesthood and God's Blessing

THE LEVITICAL PRIESTHOOD HAD the responsibility to bless the people; this act demonstrates a fundamental awareness of God's mission and was rooted in costly obedience. This chapter will start by defining "blessing" along the lines of its relational and missional connotations, then having done this proceed to look at the priesthood and their role in blessing the people.

THE RELATIONAL BASIS OF BLESSING

Christopher Wright Mitchell's dissertation on the meaning of the Hebrew word *BRK*, was a significant breakthrough in biblical theology.[1] Previous to this, understandings of "blessing," where a person is being blessed, were dominated by the works of Pedersen, Mowinckel, and Hempel.[2] For these early twentieth-century theologians, blessing had to do with primitive conceptions of the transference of power.

1. Wright Mitchell, *Meaning of BRK*.
2. Pedersen, *Israel*; Mowinckel, *Segen und Fluch*; Hempel, *Die Israelischen Ansauusnen*.

Mitchell freed the biblical concept of blessing from the realm of magic by exposing the discussion to contemporary thinking on speech-act semantics, and his findings are now well accepted. He proposed that there are two forms of blessing: illocutionary, which are descriptive, and perlocutionary, which become effective in the act of uttering them.

Illocutionary blessings, which make up the majority of cases in the Old Testament, describe the relationship between God and the person who is blessed. The effectiveness of such a blessing is not determined by any quality possessed by the person uttering the blessing but by the belief that God will fulfill what he has promised.[3]

To illustrate, one helpful example of an illocutionary blessing might be to consider the story of Balaam in Numbers 22. King Balak hires Balaam to curse the Israelites, but three times he is unable to do so and rather ends up blessing them. The King's purpose is to curse Israel, functioning as justification for his war and assurance of favor in fighting, but such a curse would have misrepresented God's relationship with his people. This is important, since God desires that this relationship be correctly perceived by the surrounding nations.[4] As a result, Balaam is unable to utter this curse, and instead ends up blessing them.

Though the vast majority of instances in Scripture, where a person is blessed, are illocutionary in nature, there are cases where illocutionary blessings contain a perlocutionary force. This will be considered further when examining the Aaronic benediction later in this chapter.

A blessing is fundamentally relational as it exposes and speaks of the relationship a person has with God; specifically it connotes a favorable relationship between God and the person blessed.[5]

---

3. Wright, *Meaning of BRK*, 82.

4. Ibid., 64.

5. Ibid., 166.

THE MISSIONAL FUNCTION OF BLESSING

To understand the concept of blessing in Scripture, it is important to appreciate its association with election and in so doing appreciate God's missional purpose in electing his people. A good place to start then is by looking at God's call of Abraham:

> Now the Lord said to Abram,
> "Go forth from your country,
> And from your relatives
> And from your father's house,
> To the land which I will show you;
> And I will make you a great nation,
> And I will bless you,
> And make your name great;
> And so you shall be a blessing;
> And I will bless those who bless you,
> And the one who curses you I will curse.
> And in you all the families of the earth will be blessed." (Gen 12:1–3)

God requires Abraham to make a costly decision: to leave his country and family and to trust solely in God. In so doing, God promises to bless not only Abraham, but also his descendants and through them bless all families.

In reading through the story of Abraham, this blessing is demonstrated through favor and benefits; economic well being, the provision of a son, protection and martial success. The reader should not be distracted though, the type of benefit is of secondary importance. The point that should not be missed is that God's blessing makes known to the recipient *and to others*, that God is favorably disposed toward the recipient.[6]

This being said, if Israel as Abraham's descendants were to live up to their calling, it is vitally important that they live as a blessed people. The law which the Israelites must obey, results in them being blessed and receiving the benefits of being in relationship with

6. Ibid., 165.

God (Deut 28). This law, though in some ways costly to follow, is freely given as an act of grace, not because of the Israelites' own righteousness but so that other nations could see and glorify the one true God (Deut 4:6).

THE COST TO BEING BLESSED

Just as Abraham had to act in costly obedience in order to receive God's blessing, the same is true for the kingdom of priests. This is particularly seen in Exodus 32 with the incident of the golden calf. It is due to the obedience of the Levites that they are enabled to serve the Lord, and it is their example which shows God's people what it means to be this kingdom of priests.

> Now when Moses saw that the people were out of control—for Aaron had let them get out of control to be a derision among their enemies—then Moses stood in the gate of the camp, and said, "Whoever is for the Lord, come to me!" And all the sons of Levi gathered together to him. He said to them, "Thus says the Lord, the God of Israel, 'Every man of you put his sword upon his thigh, and go back and forth from gate to gate in the camp, and kill every man his brother, and every man his friend, and every man his neighbor.'" So the sons of Levi did as Moses instructed, and about three thousand men of the people fell that day. Then Moses said, "Dedicate yourselves today to the Lord—for every man has been against his son and against his brother—in order that He may bestow a blessing upon you today." (Exod 32:25–29)

What is outlined in this passage is not a command to kill everyone, but a systematic going back and forth throughout the camp to find and kill those who were opposed to the Lord and refused to repent.[7] The Levites were the first to repent and for this reason Moses gives them the task of quashing the idolatry that was present in the community. This costly act of placing faithfulness to the Lord ahead of familial bonds and ties of friendship would

---

7. Stuart, *Exodus*, 681.

have been very challenging, but the fact that the Levites did this qualifies them for service. The point is emphasized again in Moses' blessing of the tribe of Levi.

> Of Levi he said,
> "Let Your Thummim and Your Urim belong to Your godly man,
> Whom You proved at Massah,
> With whom You contended at the waters of Meribah;
> Who said of his father and his mother,
> 'I did not consider them';
> And he did not acknowledge his brothers,
> Nor did he regard his own sons,
> For they observed Your word,
> And kept Your covenant.
> "They shall teach Your ordinances to Jacob,
> And Your law to Israel.
> They shall put incense before You,
> And whole burnt offerings on Your altar.
> "O Lord, bless his substance,
> And accept the work of his hands;
> Shatter the loins of those who rise up against him,
> And those who hate him, so that they will not rise again."
> (Deut 33:8–11)

It is precisely because they did not consider familial ties above their faithfulness to the Lord and his word that are positioned to discern God's will, to discern right from wrong, to teach and serve in a variety of ways. This directly impacts the Levite's function in blessing the people; for this responsibility required discernment as to whether the people were truly worthy to be blessed.

For the Israelites to fulfill their function as a kingdom of priests and to receive God's blessings, they must put faithfulness to the Lord above familial and tribal commitments, in imitation of the Levites. It is clear then, that Jesus' call for radical and costly commitment over and above familial ties (Matt 10:34–36), has strong roots in what had already been revealed and required.

This truth must also have a bearing on how the hereditary nature of the priesthood is understood. God certainly had an intention for the family; that it would embody his love and speak of relationship with him, yet ultimately this intention was subservient to faithful devotion. This point will be seen to be true at other points in the study as well; the hereditary nature of the priesthood is on condition of faithfulness to the Lord.

THE AARONIC BENEDICTION

The priesthood were to discern right from wrong, and were therefore best positioned to know when to bless Israel and when to rebuke them. As a result they were central in keeping the focus on God's mission and Israel's purpose of being a blessing to the nations. The well-known Aaronic benediction records the words of blessing which were to be spoken over the whole community.

> Then the Lord spoke to Moses, saying, "Speak to Aaron and to his sons, saying, 'Thus you shall bless the sons of Israel. You shall say to them:
> The Lord bless you, and keep you;
> The Lord make His face shine on you,
> And be gracious to you;
> The Lord lift up His countenance on you,
> And give you peace.'
> So they shall invoke My name on the sons of Israel, and I then will bless them." (Num 6:22–27)

A brief analysis of these verses reasserts the basic principle already put forward; that blessing is effectuated by God not by any strength that the Levites possess. In fact, God's name is invoked three times in the blessing, not for any grammatical reason but solely to emphasize this point, that it is the Lord's work.[8]

Significantly though, the benediction does not merely describe the relationship that the Israelites have with their God. Immediately afterwards an explanation is given to say that in

---

8. Cole, *Numbers*, 129.

speaking these words God will indeed bless them. This is then an illocutionary utterance which also contains perlocutionary force, because in the very act of uttering the blessing it is effectuated.[9] The Levites have been given the authority, albeit having consulted God beforehand, to bless his people and declare them fit for service in his mission.

It is clear from the passage that the name of the Lord is placed upon his people, "thus they shall invoke My name on the sons of Israel," and the missional overtones to this statement should not be overlooked. Indeed Psalm 67, which begins by echoing the benediction, further illustrates this point:

> May God be gracious to us and bless us
> and make his face shine on us—
> so that your ways may be known on earth,
> your salvation among all nations. (Ps 67:1–2)

It is plain to see then, that the Aaronic benediction had a missional function in declaring God's people to be of use in his mission; God, in revealing himself to the Israelites, also desired to use them in making his name known to others.

To close this chapter, Hezekiah's reinstitution of the Passover as recorded in 2 Chronicles 30 shall be considered. Hezekiah had just previously reorganized the temple worship, and then proceeded to call all Israel to celebrate the Passover (2 Chron 30:6–9): providing animals for sacrifice (2 Chron 30:24) and encouraging faithful Levites in their service (2 Chron 30:22).

As the people of Judah gathered to celebrate this salvific event, they were joined also by some from Israel and by resident aliens (2 Chron 30:25). Such was the magnitude of this event that the Chronicler states that nothing like this had happened since the time of David and Solomon (2 Chron 30:26). Though many of those coming from outside of Judah had not purified themselves according to the rules of the sanctuary, God hears Hezekiah's prayer and heals them, for he perceives their heart (2 Chron 30:20).

---

9. Wright, *Meaning of BRK*, 97.

So there was great joy in Jerusalem, because there was nothing like this in Jerusalem since the days of Solomon the son of David, king of Israel. Then the Levitical priests arose and blessed the people; and their voice was heard and their prayer came to his holy dwelling place, to heaven.

Now when all this was finished, all Israel who were present went out to the cities of Judah, broke the pillars in pieces, cut down the Asherim and pulled down the high places and the altars throughout all Judah and Benjamin, as well as in Ephraim and Manasseh, until they had destroyed them all. Then all the sons of Israel returned to their cities, each to his possession. (2 Chron 30:26—31:1)

Coming at the end of the festival, the priests and the Levites stand and bless the people there gathered. This included resident aliens, who shared in the Passover feast and were then blessed by the priesthood. The direct result of all of this is that idolatry is quelled.

This chapter has seen both the missional function of blessing the people and the costly obedience it entailed. A blessed people were a people who were in relationship with God and whose very lives proclaimed this God to others.

Blessing is both the consequence of costly obedience and of God's grace in forgiving and choosing to use a redeemed people. The Levites as "leaders" of God's people demonstrate that costly obedience is necessary in order for the people to be this "priestly nation."

3

The Priesthood and Worship

THERE IS OF COURSE an intrinsic link between the priesthood and Israel's sung worship. Not only do many of the psalms have their roots in the cult, as indicated by many of their titles, but the psalms also make countless references to cultic rituals.[1]

In a broad sense the entire ministry of the priesthood was an act of worship, and that being the case, the points being made regarding the missional nature of Israel's sung worship also have wider implications for this research. This chapter will supplement the rest of the study, highlighting the theology of mission which is perhaps most clearly seen in the Psalms. With the focus here being to affirm mission as central to the function and theology of the priesthood, the theme of costly participation is given less attention. This is not because worship is not costly, but because the costly dimension of worship is outlined in detail later in the study.

That the Levitical priesthood had the responsibility of leading the people of God in their sung worship, is clear evidence of the priesthood guiding the people in their missional calling and sharing their missional theology with the wider nation.

---

1. Creach, "Psalms and the Cult," 125.

THE PEDAGOGICAL ROLE OF WORSHIP

The opening lines of the Psalter read:

> How blessed is the man who does not walk in the counsel of
> the wicked,
> Nor stand in the path of sinners,
> Nor sit in the seat of scoffers!
> But his delight is in the law of the Lord,
> And in His law he meditates day and night.
> He will be like a tree firmly planted by streams of water,
> Which yields its fruit in its season
> And its leaf does not wither;
> And in whatever he does, he prospers. (Ps 1:1–3)

Psalm 1 is commonly taken to function as an introduction to
the whole corpus. The recent work of Michael Lefebvre on the relationship between the Psalms and the Pentateuch is of particular interest.[2] Lefebvre argues on the basis of linguistics and context that
the verb *hagah* which has traditionally been translated "meditate"
in Psalm 1:2, should be rendered "sing" so that the law mentioned
refers to the songs which the Psalmist sings.[3] This interpretation
also affirms the Talmudic tradition, paralleling the fivefold divi-
sion of the book of Psalms to that of the Pentateuch. In support
of this approach Lefebvre points to the song of Moses in Deuteronomy 32: having given the written law to the priesthood he then
proceeds to sing his song to all the Israelites. After recording this,
the text continues:

> Then Moses came and spoke all the words of this song
> in the hearing of the people, he, with Joshua the son of
> Nun. When Moses had finished speaking all these words
> to all Israel, he said to them, "Take to your heart all the
> words with which I am warning you today, which you
> shall command your sons to observe carefully, even all
> the words of this law. For it is not an idle word for you;
> indeed it is your life. And by this word you will prolong

---

2. Lefebvre, "Torah Meditation and the *Psalms.*"
3. Ibid., *218.*

> your days in the land, which you are about to cross the
> Jordan to possess." (Deut 32:44–47)

A striking moment in this passage comes when Moses tells the Israelites to observe the words of "this law," referring to the song he has just sung. In a culture not marked by widespread literacy and mass publishing, songs would be a means of meditating on the law.[4] As such it can be said that there is a certain relationship set up by the editor of the Psalms; in that the theology of the Psalms was thought to accurately represent the theological heart of the torah. Consequently, thinking on the Levites' role in organizing Israel's worship, must appreciate that the role was more than merely creating and playing aesthetically pleasing music, it also had a pedagogical role.

To go back to Psalm 1 for a moment, it should be noted that this psalm has the purpose of positioning the worshipper; he must think before singing judgment on himself (Ps 1:4–6), whether he is indeed like this man who yields fruit, or whether in fact he is walking the slippery road of the wicked.[5] If truly he is able to sing this song and those following, in so doing he meditates on God's law and is found to be "blessed," that is, fit to represent this God and participate in his mission.[6] By this reading, one of the primary functions of the Psalms is to shape a missional community. So the ethical, emotional and theological concerns of the book of Psalms need to be weighed in light of its broader missional purpose.

In addition to shaping the community, the Psalms also have the function of commissioning Israelites. There are a number of instances in the Psalms, where the Israelites are commissioned to share their knowledge of God with the nations:

> Oh give thanks to the Lord, call upon His name;

4. The "law" is referred to here, not as the antithesis of grace, but rather as a further act of grace, informing those already saved by God's grace how to live.

5. Wenham, *Psalms as Torah*.

6. This of course is not the only beatitude in the Psalms, the book is littered with them throughout; to mention only a few to illustrate the point, Pss 2, 3, 32, 84, 106, 112, 119, 128, 146.

> Make known His deeds among the peoples.
> Sing to Him, sing praises to Him;
> Speak of all His wonders. (Ps 105:1–2)

Just as God had made himself known through his wondrous acts, so also the Israelites were to join with him in making him known to all peoples. Indeed they were not alone in their witness but joined by all creation:

> The heavens declare His righteousness,
> And all the peoples have seen His glory. (Ps 97:6)

If it is to be supposed that the Israelites had no prerogative to make their God known to the nations, these verses which instruct them to do so, need to be rationalized away. Moreover some theological explanation should be expected, as to why all creation tells of God's greatness to the nations, with the exception of the Israelites.

WORSHIP AND EVANGELISM

So far in this chapter, only the pedagogical role of the book of Psalms in relation to the Israelites has been considered. A full treatment of this topic however needs to reflect upon the pedagogical role of worship *to the nations*. To appreciate this, it is well to start by recognizing that the law is missional in and of itself.

> And it will come about in the last days
> That the mountain of the house of the Lord
> Will be established as the chief of the mountains.
> It will be raised above the hills,
> And the peoples will stream to it.
> Many nations will come and say,
> "Come and let us go up to the mountain of the Lord
> And to the house of the God of Jacob,
> That He may teach us about His ways
> And that we may walk in His paths."
> For from Zion will go forth the law,

> Even the word of the Lord from Jerusalem.
> And He will judge between many peoples
> And render decisions for mighty, distant nations.
> Then they will hammer their swords into plowshares
> And their spears into pruning hooks;
> Nation will not lift up sword against nation,
> And never again will they train for war. (Mic 4:1–3)

This passage in Micah makes an extraordinary claim; the law will go out from Zion and cause the peoples to come and worship God there. The giving of the law was an act of grace which communicated good news, and contained a message for all peoples. This point is very clearly evident in the Psalms, because a number of them are actually addressed to the nations.

A good example of this is Psalm 47. This psalm together with Psalms 46 and 48 are eschatological in focus. They share a Zion theology similar to that of Micah 4 and point forward to the messianic fulfillment of hope.

> O clap your hands, all peoples;
> Shout to God with the voice of joy.
> For the Lord Most High is to be feared,
> A great King over all the earth.
> He subdues peoples under us
> And nations under our feet.
> He chooses our inheritance for us,
> The glory of Jacob whom He loves. Selah.
> God has ascended with a shout,
> The Lord, with the sound of a trumpet.
> Sing praises to God, sing praises;
> Sing praises to our King, sing praises.
> For God is the King of all the earth;
> Sing praises with a skillful psalm.
> God reigns over the nations,
> God sits on His holy throne.
> The princes of the people have assembled themselves as the people of the God of Abraham,

For the shields of the earth belong to God;
He is highly exalted. (Ps 47)

This psalm does more than just call the nations to worship the Lord; it pictures the people of God as being made up of people from the nations. Now Psalm 47 comes after a declaration of God's judgment of the nations, who are opposed to the city of God (Ps 46:6), so it would not be appropriate then to emphasize only the message of inclusion or the message of exclusion; the message of salvation or the message of judgment; they come together and in some ways are two sides of the same coin.

Another example of a psalm addressing the nations is David's song found in 1 Chronicles 16. This song is echoed in a few psalms, most explicitly in Psalm 96, and clearly had quite an influence on Israel's worship. David's song starts with a call for the Israelites to make known God's deeds to the nations and then moves to address the nations themselves.

Oh give thanks to the Lord, call upon His name;
Make known His deeds among the peoples.
Sing to Him, sing praises to Him;
Speak of all His wonders.

Sing to the Lord, all the earth;
Proclaim good tidings of His salvation from day to day.
Tell of His glory among the nations,
His wonderful deeds among all the peoples.
For great is the Lord, and greatly to be praised;
He also is to be feared above all gods.
For all the gods of the peoples are idols,
But the Lord made the heavens.
Splendor and majesty are before Him,
Strength and joy are in His place.
Ascribe to the Lord, O families of the peoples,
Ascribe to the Lord glory and strength.
Ascribe to the Lord the glory due His name;
Bring an offering, and come before Him;
Worship the Lord in holy array. (1 Chron 16:8–9, 23–29)

The context of David's song is the bringing of the ark of the covenant to Jerusalem, something which only the Levites are allowed to do, and the appointing of Asaph and other Levites to offer songs of worship. The ark of the covenant which bears testament to the law causes David to sing this song which calls all the nations to worship. Again David is joined in this call not only by the Israelites but also all of creation. So it is evident once again that the missional nature of God's law, cannot be detached from the missional nature of Israel's worship. The ark of the covenant is brought to Jerusalem and the missional purpose of this law is not missed by David.

The story of Jehoshaphat and the deliverance of Judah found in 2 Chronicles 20 provides a fitting reflection to close this chapter on worship. The story begins with news that the Moabites, the Ammonites and some of the Meunites plan to fight against Jehoshaphat. When he hears this, Jehoshaphat is afraid, prays and calls on the people of God to fast. When the people of Judah then gather together, God's spirit falls on Jahaziel a Levite of the line of Asaph. Jehaziel instructs the people what to do, telling them not to be afraid because it is God's battle, not theirs. The story then continues:

> They rose early in the morning and went out to the wilderness of Tekoa; and when they went out, Jehoshaphat stood and said, "Listen to me, O Judah and inhabitants of Jerusalem, put your trust in the Lord your God and you will be established. Put your trust in His prophets and succeed." When he had consulted with the people, he appointed those who sang to the Lord and those who praised him in holy attire, as they went out before the army and said, "Give thanks to the Lord, for His lovingkindness is everlasting." When they began singing and praising, the Lord set ambushes against the sons of Ammon, Moab and Mount Seir, who had come against Judah; so they were routed. For the sons of Ammon and Moab rose up against the inhabitants of Mount Seir destroying them completely; and when they had finished

with the inhabitants of Seir, they helped to destroy one
another. (2 Chron 20:20–23)

The story then concludes with God's people returning to
Jerusalem in praise and song, and stating that when the nations
heard about what God had done, the fear of the Lord came upon
them (2 Chron 20:29).

This story illustrates a number of points that have already observed in this chapter about the theology of worship. First, mission
is something which belongs to God, and which the people of God
can participate in through worship. Second, God is seen to be at
work in judging the nations and causing them to fear him, actions
which come hand in hand and cannot be separated. Finally, it is
again seen that God chooses to use Judah's worship in order to
reveal himself, for it is when the Levites led them the people in
worship that God set the ambush.

4

The Priesthood as Teachers
of the Law

IT IS WIDELY UNDERSTOOD that one of the key roles of the Levitical priesthood was to teach the law,[1] which in its broadest sense might also entail the discerning of God's will and administering their judicial responsibilities. This chapter will examine how the priestly role of "teacher" would inform and guide Israel in her mission to the nations.

The claim that Israel had a responsibility to teach the nations was already put forward in the introduction; that the nation as a kingdom of priests (Exod 19:6) had a priestly function in teaching the law to all peoples. The truth of this claim need not be determined by looking at the frequency of such activity in the Old Testament corpus, because much of Israel's history is a corruption of God's intention for them. Just as the Levites were to make known God's torah to every demographic in Israel, so Israel as the "royal priesthood" should make this teaching known to every nation in every language.[2] If such an idea is found to be shocking, it

1. While this was primarily the task given to the priests, they were assisted in it by the Levites (e.g., Neh 9; 2 Chron 17).

2. Hamlin, *Inheriting the Land*, 151. That the law should and could be

is perhaps, because the reader is more familiar with what Israel actually did than he is familiar with the vision of what they should have done.

God intended the priesthood to be a source of knowledge for Israel, in the same way that Israel was to be God's informant to the nations. As shall be evidenced in this chapter, the priesthood as administers of the law were models for the entire nation, such that when the priesthood were unfaithful to God in their teaching, Israel stood little chance of fulfilling their role in God's mission.

THE JUDGMENT OF UNFAITHFUL TEACHERS

The prophets ministering just prior to the Israel's exile did not hesitate to proclaim prophetic words of judgment on the priesthood, for the worship of the Lord had been converted into blatant paganism as a consequence of the priests' apostasy. The conduct of the priest had descended into the drinking and prostitution closely associated with idolatrous worship.[3] This being the case, the prophet Hosea speaks God's judgment:

> My people are destroyed for lack of knowledge.
> Because you have rejected knowledge,
> I also will reject you from being My priest.
> Since you have forgotten the law of your God,
> I also will forget your children.
> The more they multiplied, the more they sinned against Me;
> I will change their glory into shame.
> They feed on the sin of My people
> And direct their desire toward their iniquity.
> And it will be, like people, like priest;
> So I will punish them for their ways
> And repay them for their deeds.
> They will eat, but not have enough;
> They will play the harlot, but not increase,

---

translated, such that the hearers might understand, is evidenced in Neh 8.

3. Smith, *Hosea, Amos, Micah*, 86.

> Because they have stopped giving heed to the Lord.
> Harlotry, wine and new wine take away the understanding.
> My people consult their wooden idol, and their diviner's wand informs them;
> For a spirit of harlotry has led them astray,
> And they have played the harlot, departing from their God.
> They offer sacrifices on the tops of the mountains
> And burn incense on the hills,
> Under oak, poplar and terebinth,
> Because their shade is pleasant.
> Therefore your daughters play the harlot
> And your brides commit adultery. (Hos 4:6–13)

Focal to Hosea's judgment is the priest's failure to teach the law; the testimony of what God had done and who he was. The wellbeing of the law was as precious to God as children to a parent (Hos 4:6), and the failure to teach it results not only in the rejection of the priests but also the punishment of the nation (Hos 4:6). The role of the priest then was pivotal, when they were faithful to their calling, God's love would be made known (Hos 4:1), but when they stumbled the rest of Israel were certain to stumble with them. It is important to note that the priests' faithfulness does not only affect the people's "spiritual well-being" but equally affects their social health. The unfaithfulness of the priest is mirrored by the Israelites' faithlessness to their familial responsibilities (Hos 4:13–14). Faithfulness to teaching God's law was therefore not merely a commitment made to an abstract theology, but resulted in an outward demonstration of God's love to others.

In this passage God announces that he will forget the priests' children, which considering the hereditary nature of the priesthood would elicit their destruction. This raises a problem, not least because elsewhere as shall be seen, God promises to continue his covenant with the Levitical priesthood forever. This issue will come up again when interpreting the next passage in Malachi, but here in Hosea at least, it can certainly be said that God's covenant with the Levites was in some way conditional to their obedience. Such obedience was a requirement to being involved in God's mission, and there are, as here, other instances when a priest's disobedience disqualifies them from participation (e.g., Lev 10; 1 Sam 2:27ff). Malachi similarly pronounces judgment on the Levites for failing to teach God's law:

> "Behold, I am going to rebuke your offspring, and I will spread refuse on your faces, the refuse of your feasts; and you will be taken away with it. Then you will know that I have sent this commandment to you, that My covenant may continue with Levi," says the Lord of hosts. "My covenant with him was one of life and peace, and I gave them to him as an object of reverence; so he revered Me and stood in awe of My name. True instruction was in his mouth and unrighteousness was not found on his lips; he walked with Me in peace and uprightness, and he turned many back from iniquity. For the lips of a priest should preserve knowledge, and men should seek instruction from his mouth; for he is the messenger of the Lord of hosts. But as for you, you have turned aside from the way; you have caused many to stumble by the instruction; you have corrupted the covenant of Levi," says the Lord of hosts. "So I also have made you despised and abased before all the people, just as you are not keeping My ways but are showing partiality in the instruction." (Mal 2:3–9)

In the same way that the priests had despised the Lord, so God would also make them despised and abased before the people. Here it is seen that their impartiality in teaching the law and upholding justice constituted the priesthood's failure. Although the precise judicial function of the Levitical priest is not completely clear, they would undoubtedly have made pronouncements on religious affairs (Lev 10:10; 13:1—14:57). As well as this there is some additional evidence that they also operated in a wider legal context (Deut 21:5; Ezek 44:24). The priesthood operating in an enclavist society were not meant to show partiality, but rather protect and uphold the weakest and most vulnerable, even if needs be at their own expense. Yet when they opted for their own comfort and prosperity above God's law (e.g., Hos 4:12), God caused them to be brought low before the people.

The priesthood's pride fueled a nationalism by which Israel thought of itself as divinely appointed above the nations. This became not only an obstruction to the priests' ability to teach, it also distracted the nation away from their universal mission.

Just as Hosea, at the time of his ministering, proclaimed God's rejection of the priestly line, so Malachi speaking at a later time also delivers a similar message. However Malachi makes it clear that the Lord's covenant with Levi would continue (Mal 2:4). Theirs was a covenant of "life and peace," and Israel under their jurisdiction was to be an embodiment of this covenant. Without faithful obedience though, this life and peace could not be channeled through the people to the surrounding nations.

To illustrate this point, one image of the Priests and Levites administering their function correctly can be seen when the nation returned from exile. Ezra reads the law (Neh 8), the people repent (Neh 9) and affirm their covenant commitments (Neh 10). Yet joined there with the ethnic Israelites were those who had separated themselves from the "peoples of the lands" and joined the covenant community (Neh 10:28). The law therefore is seen to be for the nations also, bringing them to a point of repentance and worship.

God's rejection of the priesthood needs then to be viewed in the light of his commitment of love to Israel and the world. Yet in order for God to be faithful to his covenant with Levi and also reject the line of those unfaithful priests, he must either reserve a remnant of faithful priests or graft other faithful individuals into the priesthood. In fact there is evidence of both; in the book of Nehemiah, God does indeed set aside a faithful remnant. Yet it is also seen with the election of Samuel (1 Sam 2) that God is able to graft others in.

RAISING UP A FAITHFUL TEACHER

The Philistines drew up in battle array to meet Israel. When the battle spread, Israel was defeated before the Philistines who killed about four thousand men on the battlefield. When the people came into the camp, the elders of Israel said, "Why has the Lord defeated us today before the Philistines? Let us take to ourselves from Shiloh the ark of the covenant of the Lord, that it may come among us and deliver us from the power of our enemies." So the people sent to Shiloh, and from there they carried the ark of the covenant of the Lord of hosts who sits above the cherubim; and the two sons of Eli, Hophni and Phinehas, were there with the ark of the covenant of God.

As the ark of the covenant of the Lord came into the camp, all Israel shouted with a great shout, so that the earth resounded. When the Philistines heard the noise of the shout, they said, "What does the noise of this great shout in the camp of the Hebrews mean?" Then they understood that the ark of the Lord had come into the camp. The Philistines were afraid, for they said, "God has come into the camp." And they said, "Woe to us! For nothing like this has happened before. Woe to us! Who shall deliver us from the hand of these mighty gods? These are the gods who smote the Egyptians with all kinds of plagues in the wilderness. Take courage and be men, O Philistines, or you will become slaves to the Hebrews, as they have been slaves to you; therefore, be men and fight."

So the Philistines fought and Israel was defeated, and every man fled to his tent; and the slaughter was very great, for there fell of Israel thirty thousand foot soldiers. And the ark of God was taken; and the two sons of Eli, Hophni and Phinehas, died. (1 Sam 4:2–11)

The ark of the covenant contained three items: the tablets of stone from Sinai, a jar of manna from the wilderness and Aaron's rod which budded. It stood as continuing reminder of God's teaching (the tablets), provision (the manna) and salvation (the rod) for them, and gave solid evidence of God's revealed character.[4] The ark signified God's presence with his people both past and present and its loss symbolized the defeat of the Lord. Indeed the most devastating aspect recorded in this account is the humiliation of the Lord at the hands of Israel's enemies.[5] In the following chapter, the Philistines placed the ark at the foot of Dagon their god, only to see the statue of Dagon fall face down before the ark (1 Sam 5:1–5). When it became apparent to the Philistines, that they were being inflicted with tumors because of their possession of the ark, they eventually returned the ark to Israel (1 Sam 6).

That God chose to humiliate himself rather than assume the role that the Israelites wanted, is very significant. In this story, God refuses to be the lucky mascot of Israel's nationalistic triumphalism. Instead he chooses to reveal himself to the Philistines in meekness and is willing to be humiliated in so doing.[6] The elders of Israel claim to want to discern God's will (1 Sam 4:3), yet the speed of their actions suggests that their question was not a genuine enquiry.[7] Even still, it was ultimately the responsibility of the priests to enquire of the Lord and instruct the elders accordingly. Hophni and Phineas though neglect to enquire of God; possibly still reveling in their role as guardians of the ark and expecting a handsome payment.[8] God's instruction is reduced to a good luck charm, and the priests who ironically fear the Lord less than the priests of Dagon (1 Sam 5:5) face God's judgment. In light of the Levites' failure to instruct, God himself reveals his nature to both Israel and the Philistines, with the same humility that is required of the priesthood.

---

4. There is some discussion surrounding 1 Kgs 8:9 as to whether these items were truly there contained. However this verse in Kings does not necessarily contradict the testimony of other passages; Exod 16:33–34, Num 17:10, Heb 9:3–4.

5. Brueggemann, *First and Second Samuel*, 45.

6. Though it is our purpose here to underline God's act of weakness, it is ultimately his strength and triumph over Dagon which gives theological import to his weakness.

7. Firth, *1 & 2 Samuel*, 85.

8. Evans, *Message of Samuel*, 44.

Despite the passing of many generations, the story of the exodus and God's redemption of Israel from the hand of the Egyptians is known to the Philistines and is treated as a historical event. Even their somewhat misinformed account of the exodus story leads them to show more fear for God than the priests do. Nevertheless, in spite of Israel's disobedience, God is intent on revealing himself to the Philistines just as he had done to Pharaoh before. Unlike Pharaoh, however, the Philistines choose not to harden their hearts (1 Sam 6:6); they offer sacrifices to God and are healed of their tumors as a result (1 Sam 6:4). This God of power who humiliates himself out of love for the nations was meant to be professed and embodied in the priests' witness. It was precisely because Eli's sons were not committed to this cause, that God vows to cut them off and raise up another faithful priest in their stead (1 Sam 2:35).

First Samuel follows on chronologically from the book of Judges which details Israel's descent into their ever rising sinfulness, despite God's provision of the judges. This regression culminated in the story of the Levite and his concubine and the resulting war with the tribe of Benjamin. At the beginning of first Samuel, both Israel and their priesthood have remained in their rebellious state. Samuel the instrument of God's faithfulness and love is contrasted throughout the opening chapters with Hophni and Phineas the sons of Eli the priest, who are even pictured lying with women who serve outside the tent of meeting (1 Sam 2:22). In the context of the unfaithfulness of Eli's sons, God vows to raise up a faithful priest (1 Sam 2:35), as a replacement. This has often been taken to be a reference to the Zadokite priesthood, because of the reference back to this prophecy in 1 Kings 2:27. Nevertheless, the constant references to Samuel and the following chapter which seeks to legitimate this new leadership would encourage a reading which includes him.[9] Perhaps it is best to say that the succession begins with Samuel, but has implications which are echoed elsewhere in Scripture.

Throughout this chapter it has been noted that God sometimes rejects the priestly line, when they are disobedient and

---

9. Fishbane, "1 Samuel 3," 191.

neglect their duties of teaching his people. Yet it is seen with the installment of Samuel, an Ephraimite, that God is also able to graft others into the priesthood.[10] An understanding that God was able to graft others in, helps to shed light on Isaiah's prophecy that even Gentiles will serve as priests and Levites.

> Then they shall bring all your brethren from all the nations as a grain offering to the Lord, on horses, in chariots, in litters, on mules and on camels, to My holy mountain Jerusalem," says the Lord, "just as the sons of Israel bring their grain offering in a clean vessel to the house of the Lord. I will also take some of them for priests and for Levites," says the Lord. (Isa 66:20–21)

As a consequence of the coming of the "anointed one" (Isa 61:6) Israel will again be restored to being a priestly people.[11] Yet these verses make it clear that it won't just be Israelites who make up the people of God and their priesthood, for they will also be joined by Gentiles. These verses therefore, contain the ultimate image of inclusiveness, for if a Gentile could become a Levitical priest he could not be excluded from anything.[12] Isaiah's message would have been very shocking to his listeners, and demanded a radically different attitude both toward the priesthood and toward foreigners than his audience held; for it was always God's intention that the Gentiles would join with Israel in their worship.

This chapter has found that for the priesthood to teach God's law they must suffer humility, even as God does in revealing

10. Some discussion has arisen over whether Samuel was a Levite or an Ephraimite. 1 Chron 6, indicates that Samuel and his father were Levites, but 1 Sam 1 has no interest in his Levitical heritage, if indeed he had any, and informs us that he is from Ephraim (Firth, *1 & 2 Samuel*, 54). This means that either Samuel was a Levite whose family came from Ephraim or he was an Ephraimite who was grafted into the Levitical priesthood (Thompson, *1, 2 Chronicles*, 86). It is more probable though that Samuel came from the tribe of Ephraim, for in Judg 17:7 the Levite, who came from the land of Judah, is called a Levite not an Ephraimite (Driver, *Notes on the Hebrew Text*, 4). It seems then that Samuel was not ransomed according to the command given in Num 8, and therefore belonged to the Levites.

11. Motyer, *Prophecy of Isaiah*, 542.

12. Oswalt, *Book of Isaiah*, 690.

himself. They must submit themselves to God's word and command, not their own sinful desires or the desires of others which would promote lawlessness and injustice. Just as was seen in the case of Samuel, God is prepared to graft non-Levites into the priesthood, in order to humble a puffed up priesthood and remind the people of their missional identity. This missional identity was marked by servitude and humility, for such was the character of their God in revealing himself. When the Levites neglected God's law, the whole nation also lost sight of God's word and mission, becoming instead proud and inward looking.

5

The Priesthood and Sanctification

ISRAEL WAS TO BE a "holy nation" (Exod 19:6), which would stand as a testimony to the surrounding nations of God's own holiness. Without holiness therefore, Israel could not measure up to the missional role given to them.[1] In this section it shall be argued that holiness is a positioning of the self before God, to be of use in his mission; specifically this requires a posture of servitude and suffering.

Holiness is often held to be a goal or ideal to be striven for, recently however Nobuyoshi Kiuchi has proposed that the term has to do with the absence of the egocentric nature.[2] Kiuchi recognized that the relationship of holiness with death suggests that the essence of holiness lies in death and specifically, he contends, the death of the egocentric nature.[3] By this definition of holiness, the priesthood were called to be the epitome of selflessness for

---

1. Wright, *Mission of God*, 333.
2. Kiuchi, *Leviticus*, 28.
3. Ibid., 40.

the people, who modeled the people's selfless ministry to the surrounding nations.[4]

It was not only people however who could be holy; it was also places, there is some connection between the two. Douglas has already shown that God's sanctuary corresponds to the worshipper,[5] and building on this Kiuchi argues that the holiness attached to a place is connected to the selflessness required of the worshipper.[6] The more holy the place, the more selflessness is required. The holy of holies in this light, becomes representative of the innermost part of the worshipper, where the restrictions on entering it are indicative of the difficulty in acquiring such a level of selflessness.

In addition to places which were to be holy, the priesthood were also responsible for administering certain times which were holy (Lev 23). These were times when the people would humble themselves before their God. There is for instance the Day of Atonement, where the Israelites were to "afflict themselves," a strong expression which entailed the cessation from work and possibly a time of fasting.[7] So serious in fact was this command, that anyone who failed to afflict himself on that day was to be cut off from the people (Lev 23:29). By failing to humble oneself before God, that individual disqualified himself from this holy nation.

Holiness is related to the community's relationship with God, and this relationship served as a witness to the nations. The intention being that Israel's humility and selflessness would bear testimony of a selflessly compassionate God, who in the majesty of his holiness demanded worship.

---

4. A full evaluation of Kiuchi's understanding of holiness would also require an examination of his distinguishing between the Hebrew words for person, man and soul. Such a discussion would be out of place here, but has been capably put forward in Kiuchi's commentary on Leviticus.

5. Douglas, *Leviticus as Literature*, 134.

6. Kiuchi, *Leviticus*, 43.

7. Hartley, *Leviticus*, 223.

THE NATURE OF HOLINESS

To be holy was a hazardous occupation. This section will explore this statement further, by considering the texts of Leviticus 6 and Ezekiel 44.

> Now this is the law of the grain offering: the sons of Aaron shall present it before the Lord in front of the altar . . . It shall not be baked with leaven. I have given it as their share from My offerings by fire; it is most holy, like the sin offering and the guilt offering. Every male among the sons of Aaron may eat it; it is a permanent ordinance throughout your generations, from the offerings by fire to the Lord. Whoever touches them will become consecrated. (Lev 6:14, 17, 18)

Much discussion surrounds the last phrase in particular, as to whether it should be interpreted to mean; those (priests) who touch the portion must be holy for otherwise they will desecrate it, or whether it means that all who touch it will become holy through contact with it.[8] One commentator, Demarest, points to Haggai 2:11–13, which suggests that holiness is not contagious, thereby arguing that Leviticus 6:18 is meant as a warning to the priests to be meticulous in following the prescribed regulations.[9] Even still it would seem to fit the passage in Leviticus better if it was taken to be a warning to lay persons, for it would appear redundant to tell the priests that to touch it they must be holy.[10] In interpreting Leviticus 6:18 though, it should be understood that its purpose is not to put forward a theology of contagious holiness, but rather the expression serves as a formula forewarning God's judgment.[11] As such it concerns an alteration in the individual's posture toward

8. Tidball, *Message of Leviticus*, 99.

9. Demarest, *Leviticus*, 74.

10. Wenham, *Book of Leviticus*, 121. Consequently some have suggested that the idea that holiness could not be transmitted is postexilic (Harrison, *Leviticus*, 74). Aside from the difficulties involved in translating Lev 6:18 in this way, there is little reason for us to think this on the basis of context.

11. Budd, *Leviticus*, 111.

God not the contagion of a material matter.[12] It is striking in this passage that holiness is seen as something dangerous, and symptomatic of God's judgment.[13] Yet this connection between holiness and being set aside to suffer is also found in other passages as well:

> The Levites who went far from Me when Israel went astray, who went astray from Me after their idols, shall bear the punishment for their iniquity. Yet they shall be ministers in My sanctuary, having oversight at the gates of the house and ministering in the house; they shall slaughter the burnt offering and the sacrifice for the people, and they shall stand before them to minister to them. (Ezek 44:10–11)

Coming immediately after the Lord's rebuke of the Levites for allowing foreigners into the temple, this passage rehabilitates the Levitical priesthood to their former role. While some have interpreted this passage to imply the punishment and demotion of the Levites, restricting their influence,[14] the Levites ministry is actually being extended to include the slaughtering of the sacrifices as well.[15]

Wellhausen drew heavily on this passage for his explication of Israel's social history.[16] In Ezekiel 44, he believed there to be evidence of a struggle for power between the Levitical and Zadokite priesthoods, which came to a head during the exilic period. To be clear, there is no evidence to suggest that all the Levites previously functioned as priests before the exile, as Wellhausen supposes. Nor is there evidence to suggest that the Zadokites and the Levites were separate entities, for the Zadokites are also identified as Levites (Ezek 44:15). A hierarchy in sanctity does not necessitate a hierarchy in power, and there is no reason to think that there was a power struggle within the priesthood at the time of the exile.[17]

12. Kiuchi, *Leviticus*, 125.

13. Allen, *Ezekiel 20–48*, 263.

14. Wevers, *Ezekiel*, 220.

15. Duguid, *Ezekiel*, 502.

16. Wellhausen, *Prolegomena to the History of Ancient Israel*, 123.

17. Block, *Book of Ezekiel*, 571.

Once such misreadings of the passage have been abandoned, it becomes clear that this is not a punitive demotion of the Levites but a confirmation of their subordinate status even in spite of their sin.[18] In the midst of this gracious act of reinstatement, however, come the condemning words "they shall bear the punishment of their iniquity." One way of interpreting this is, to read this phrase intertextually as echoing the words of Numbers 18:1 which speaks of the priests bearing their own guilt.[19] Although it is true that the word for "iniquity" is different to the word used in Numbers for "guilt," the likelihood is that there is an echo due to the shared theme of sacrifice.

From these passages (Num 18:1; Lev 6:18, Ezek 44:11) it is evident that the Levites function as "spiritual lightning conductors"[20] on behalf of the nation. God's wrath is transferred from the people onto the priesthood, who are capable of being an acceptable sacrifice before God. With this in mind God's warning in Leviticus 6:18 makes sense: those who touch the grain offering become consecrated. For to be holy is to be open to God's wrath, yet unless one is part of the priesthood, he is incapable of being a pleasing sacrifice to God.[21] As for the Levites, their offering of themselves can only be acceptable if they remain holy and unblemished, which according to the definition of holiness outlined above is only made possible by their selfless ministry.

This understanding of holiness can also be seen in the story of Uzzah (2 Sam 6). Uzzah was one of the men carrying the Ark to Jerusalem after it had been returned by the Philistines. When the oxen stumbled however Uzzah reached out and touched the Ark and was struck down dead. As a consequence when David later brought the Ark to Jerusalem sacrifices were offered after every six steps.

Holiness is a dangerous occupation because it is so closely associated with sacrifice and God's judgment. This naturally leads on

---

18. Lamar, *Ezekiel*, 394.
19. Duke, "Punishment or Restoration?," 66.
20. Milgrom, *Encroacher and the Levite*, 31.
21. Wenham, *Book of Leviticus*, 121.

to considering the place of sacrifice in the theology of the priesthood. There are two sides to this; first to look at the priesthood as a sacrificial offering themselves, which ties into the discussion above on Leviticus 6 and Ezekiel 44, and second to look at their role of offering sacrifices on behalf of others.

THE PRIESTHOOD AS A HOLY SACRIFICE

The relationship between the priesthood's holiness and their role as a sacrifice for the nation is clearly and most obviously seen in their consecration ceremony.

> The Lord spoke to Moses, saying, "Take the Levites from among the sons of Israel and cleanse them. Thus you shall do to them, for their cleansing: sprinkle purifying water on them, and let them use a razor over their whole body and wash their clothes, and they will be clean. Then let them take a bull with its grain offering, fine flour mixed with oil; and a second bull you shall take for a sin offering. So you shall present the Levites before the tent of meeting. You shall also assemble the whole congregation of the sons of Israel, and present the Levites before the Lord; and the sons of Israel shall lay their hands on the Levites. Aaron then shall present the Levites before the Lord as a wave offering from the sons of Israel, that they may qualify to perform the service of the Lord. Now the Levites shall lay their hands on the heads of the bulls; then offer the one for a sin offering and the other for a burnt offering to the Lord, to make atonement for the Levites. You shall have the Levites stand before Aaron and before his sons so as to present them as a wave offering to the Lord." (Num 8:5–13)

This consecration ceremony which presented the Levites as an offering, qualified them for service. The Levites' devotion is ultimately to God who has assigned them to serve under the jurisdiction of the priests.[22] Just as an animal being sacrificed is representative of the offerer, so also the Levites were representative

---

22. Levine, *Numbers 1–20*, 278.

of the whole nation. This is demonstrated within the ceremony when the Israelites lay their hands on the Levites as the Levites are offered to the Lord. It should also be noted that through this wave offering, the Levites redeem Israel's firstborn; a point which will be explored further in the next chapter.[23]

An understanding that the Levitical priesthood were themselves meant to be a holy sacrifice on behalf of the people, helps in reflecting theologically upon the genealogical records contained in Ezra 2–3 and Nehemiah 7.

Before the exile, David had divided the priesthood, according to the heads of twenty-four Levitical families, with each taking different responsibilities (1 Chron 24). Among the home comers though there were only four of these families present, which meant that the priestly tasks had to be redistributed.[24] It seems that although most Jewish families kept records of their genealogies (1 Chron 5:17), some of these records had been lost in the exilic period. In the case of the Levites, those unable to prove their lineage were not permitted to function as priests (Ezra 2:62).

Many readers struggle to make sense of the genealogical records in Ezra; aside from making an uninviting read, it seems to be suggestive of racial exclusivism.[25] Indeed the concern for pedigree certainly seems to have blossomed into a sense of superiority by the time of the New Testament; making it difficult for the Christian to square these passages with Jesus' words of criticism (e.g., Matt 3:9).[26] In biblical scholarship also, the hereditary nature of the priesthood has often been misconstrued as the outworking of "tribal politics,"[27] and labeled "elitist."[28]

---

23. The wave offering constituted part of a number of sacrificial ceremonies; the burnt, fellowship and atonement offering, but it is not clear which is being made reference to here (Cole, *Numbers*, 152). While discussion surrounds the symbolic value of the wave offering, it seems well to see it as part of the sacrifice which presents the offering to God.

24. Kidner, *Ezra and Nehemiah*, 39.

25. Williamson, *Ezra, Nehemiah*, 38.

26. Kidner, *Ezra and Nehemiah*, 41.

27. Tiemeyer, *Priestly Rites and Prophetic Rage*, 198.

28. Milgrom, *Leviticus 1–16*, 53.

As already noted, the priesthood was not rigidly hereditary; people could be incorporated into it and cut off from it. In what sense and for what purpose then do these texts record and value the genealogies of the priests? A lineage which legitimized a Levite's true descent from Levi, notions the idea that the Levites were to be an unblemished offering on behalf of the people. This concept is evidenced by the fact that the priests number about a tenth of the returnees,[29] the portion of Israel's tithe and offering to God, and that those excluded because they could not prove their lineage, were done so because this made them 'unclean' (Ezra 2:62). The genealogies in Ezra therefore demonstrate that God had not abandoned his covenant with the Levites: he was committed to using them in his mission to the world, even as he had determined to do in Numbers 8. Yet their ministry must operate within the metaphor of being an unblemished sacrifice.

OFFERING SACRIFICES ON BEHALF OF THE PEOPLE

One of the fundamental features in offering a sacrifice was that it had to be costly.[30] The animal being sacrificed could not be wild game, but had to be reared (Lev 1:2). This point can also be seen in the story of 2 Samuel 24, where David desires to build an altar on the threshing floor belonging to Araunah. Araunah offers to give it as a gift to David, but David insists on buying it, saying, "I will not offer burnt offerings to the Lord My God which cost me nothing" (2 Sam 24:24). Perhaps it is difficult for the modern reader to appreciate the cost involved in offering a portion of livelihood as a burnt offering, especially when oftentimes contemporary traditions and forms of worship are relatively cost free. Yet the Israelites also fell into the practice of cheap worship, and Isaiah spoke out against it:

> You have bought Me not sweet cane with money,

29. Blenkinsopp, *Gibeon and Israel*, 98.
30. Wenham, *Book of Leviticus*, 51.

> Nor have you filled Me with the fat of your sacrifices;
> Rather you have burdened Me with your sins,
> You have wearied Me with your iniquities. (Isa 43:24)

The Israelites had not been paying the expense which God required (Isa 43:24a). As a result their worship had become distorted and perverse, lacking any real devotion.

As noted at the beginning of this chapter, it is holiness which allows Israel to participate in their missional identity. Holiness can only be achieved through selfless submission in dependence to God, an act accomplished through the faithful and God-fearing practice of offering of a costly sacrifice. As such the priesthood were facilitators of God's mission, enabling and equipping the people of God to submit their lives in devotion to and witness of a holy God.

The idea that a sacrifice was food for God was not prominent in Israel, as it was for the nations which surrounded her. Rather a sacrifice was food for human beings which generated community and fellowship.[31] The worship of God and the offerer's humility were the basis of unity and fellowship. The sacrifice which symbolized the offerer's own life was the result of selfless devotion, and thereby the foundation for reconciliation both to God and to others in society. It might well be said that in the same way the Levites offered sacrifices for the purpose of reconciliation, so the priestly nation of Israel was to work for reconciliation amongst the nations.[32]

Holiness as Enacted Prophecy

The priesthood's role was to represent God's own nature and rule to the nations. Therefore it is not surprising that the Messiah, who would be both man and God (Isa 9:6), would have own his rule prefigured by the selfless rule of the Levitical priesthood:

---

31. Miller, *Religion of Ancient Israel*, 128.
32. Hamlin, *Inheriting the Land*, 151.

> The angel of the Lord admonished Joshua, saying, "Thus says the Lord of hosts, 'If you will walk in my ways and if you will perform my service, then you will also govern my house and also have charge of my courts, and I will grant you free access among these who are standing here. Now listen, Joshua the high priest, you and your friends who are sitting in front of you—indeed they are men who are a symbol, for behold, I am going to bring in my servant the Branch.'" (Zech 3:6–8)

In this, Zechariah's fourth vision, the high priest Joshua is reclothed out of his filthy dress, literally "garments of excrement,"[33] with the implication that he can no longer be accused by Satan. Being restored again to the image of holiness requires that Joshua and those serving under him act accordingly; so the angel informs that if he walks in the way of the Lord then he can rightly serve in God's holy temple. For Joshua's service to be acceptable he must walk in God's ways. As was the case in Ezekiel 44, the priesthood's reinstatement has nothing to do with their own worth and everything to do with the grace and holiness of the God they serve.

Following this, the angel informs Joshua of God's intention that they are to be a symbol of the messiah's rule. Drawing upon the images used for the messiah in Isaiah, the angel makes it clear that the priesthood was to prefigure the messianic rule to the nation.

The people of Israel were to be a "holy nation," a people whose devotion would cause them to stand out from the other nations. The Levites were to model to the tribes of Israel, what such holiness looked like. More than this though, the priesthood were also chosen to lead the people into sanctification, through the offering of sacrifices. As observed, in order to enable this holy nation to fulfill its missional role, the Levites had to see and experience their service as a sacrifice.

33. Merrill, *Haggai, Zechariah, Malachi*, 121.

6

The Priesthood as an
Enslaved People

TIGHTLY CONNECTED TO THE metaphor of slavery is the metaphor depicting the Levites as a firstfruits offering. The remit of this chapter goes in some ways beyond the metaphor of slavery then because of the textual link between the "firstborn" and the "firstfruits," but this is ultimately done in order to unpack the metaphor of slavery and the costly service there implied.

The previous chapter noted that the priesthood themselves were to be an offering to God. This chapter will build upon this point to show that the Levites were as slaves before God; an image for the whole nation, reminding them of their role in God's mission.

THE LEVITES AS A GIFT

The connection between the Levites as an offering and the Levites as an enslaved people can be seen in the consecration ceremony itself.

Then after that the Levites may go in to serve the tent of meeting. But you shall cleanse them and present them as a wave offering; for they are wholly given to Me from among the sons of Israel. I have taken them for Myself instead of every first issue of the womb, the firstborn of all the sons of Israel. For every firstborn among the sons of Israel is Mine, among the men and among the animals; on the day that I struck down all the firstborn in the land of Egypt I sanctified them for Myself. But I have taken the Levites instead of every firstborn among the sons of Israel. (Num 8:15–18)

At the same time that the Israelites are presented as a wave offering, they are also spoken of as the replacement for the first born sons of Israel. This alludes back to the sin of the golden calf (Exod 32:26–9) for which the Levites were the redemption price. Initially in light of the Passover event, the firstborn of every Israelite belonged to God (Exod 13:2), but Israel's sinful rebellion (Exod 32) caused this role to be transferred onto the Levites. In the midst of Israel's rebellion, the Levites sided with the Lord, and it was for this reason that the Levites could function as the redemption fee, taking on the role of the "firstborn." This redemptive act was done on behalf of the Israelite people whereby the Levites functioned as a substitute.[1] The practice of redeeming the firstborn would surely remind the Israelites of Mount Sinai, and the gracious God who forgave them for their idolatry. This analogy would similarly aid them to reflect missionally on how this priestly nation, could enable the redemption of the nations in the midst of their rebellion to God; declaring judgment on those who would not repent and salvation on those who do in dependence upon God's grace. The stipulations regarding the redemption of the firstborn are further laid out in Numbers 3:

All the numbered men of the Levites, whom Moses and Aaron numbered at the command of the Lord by their families, every male from a month old and upward, were 22,000. Then the Lord said to Moses, "Number every

---

1. Wenham, *Numbers*, 96.

firstborn male of the sons of Israel from a month old and upward, and make a list of their names. You shall take the Levites for Me, I am the Lord, instead of all the firstborn among the sons of Israel, and the cattle of the Levites instead of all the firstborn among the cattle of the sons of Israel." So Moses numbered all the firstborn among the sons of Israel, just as the Lord had commanded him; and all the firstborn males by the number of names from a month old and upward, for their numbered men were 22,273.

Then the Lord spoke to Moses, saying, "Take the Levites instead of all the firstborn among the sons of Israel and the cattle of the Levites. And the Levites shall be Mine; I am the Lord. For the ransom of the 273 of the firstborn of the sons of Israel who are in excess beyond the Levites, you shall take five shekels apiece, per head; you shall take them in terms of the shekel of the sanctuary (the shekel is twenty gerahs), and give the money, the ransom of those who are in excess among them, to Aaron and to his sons." (Num 3:39–48)

While Numbers 3 records the inauguration of this practice, this was a continuing ordinance for every generation (Num 18:15–16), so that at the birth of every firstborn a redemption price would need to be paid for the child's ransom. As such this was not just a symbolic one off event, but the initiation of a ritual which would function as a continuing evocation to the whole of God's people; reminding the nation of who they were and what God had done for them.[2] Numbers 3 affirms the substitutionary significance of this custom; the surplus of Israelites had to be counted and paid for with a sum equivalent to what they would fetch if sold, as slaves on the open market.[3] As already alluded to in our research on Samuel, the God-fearing parent had a choice; they could either pay the redemption price, which was the equivalent of six months pay,[4] or give their child for God's service as is the case with Sam-

2. Brown, *Message of Numbers*, 37.

3. Wenham, *Numbers*, 71.

4. Ibid., 144.

son (Judg 13) and Samuel (1 Sam 1). This was essentially a lifelong Nazirite vow.[5]

That the Levites functioned as a substitute for the people in this way does not mean that the Israelites themselves were not also God's possession. In Leviticus 25, which outlines some of the manumission laws and the jubilee procedures, God makes it clear that "the sons of Israel are My servants; they are My servants whom I brought out of the land of Egypt" (Lev 25:55).

Of course the metaphor of slavery cannot be detached from God's redemptive story. God had acquired his slaves by redeeming them from Egyptian bondage.[6] They had been brought out from Egypt and the service of Egyptian gods, to work in building a nation and people which speak of the greatness of God. Having said this, Israel's slavery was a life-giving bondage to their God and not like the Egyptian slavery they experienced. It was in many ways different from that imposed on slaves by the surrounding nations. In parts of the ancient Near East for example, private citizens dedicated chattel slaves to the temple in order to secure favors from the gods.[7] In addition to the chattel slavery that existed in the surrounding nations, there was an increasing amount of debt slavery, due to a process of centralization which alienated their citizens from land.[8] Yet in Israel chattel slavery was to be nonexistent,[9] and debt slaves were to be freed, according to the jubilee regulations.[10]

The bondage to God which every Israelite was subject to, was life giving and rooted in love and grace. This point is corroborated in the biblical manumission laws, which refer to a separate class of landless Israelites.[11] These laws were not repressive, but liberating

5. Levenson, *Death and Resurrection*, 47.

6. Levine, *Leviticus*, 179.

7. Mendelsohn, *Slavery in the Ancient Near East*, 102.

8. Chirichigno, *Debt Slavery*, 35.

9. Milgrom, *Leviticus*, 304.

10. Harrison, *Leviticus*, 75.

11. Kaufman, "Reconstruction," 278.

in that they sought to support of the most vulnerable members of society.

THE LEVITES AS A MODEL FOR GIVING

The Levites were metaphorically referred to as the "firstfruits." This metaphor again connects the two themes of sacrifice and slavery, where the Levites who were "sacrificed" were also the symbolic firstfruits of the womb. The whole of Israel, the Levites and priests included, were to offer tithes and this began with the firstfruits. Though some have tried to differentiate between the tithe and the offering of the firstfruits, on the basis of who consumes the offering,[12] they are essentially connected.[13] As their use in Deuteronomy 26 would indicate, the firstfruits are best understood as an initial token payment of the tithe, and a fearful acknowledgement of their dependence upon God.[14]

In light of the relationship between tithing and the firstfruits, this section will consider the role of tithing for the nation's participation in God's mission; before returning again to the concept of the Levites as firstfruits. This will enable a more thorough understanding of the Levite's role.

It is surprising that despite the importance of tithing to Israel's life of worship, the practice is only mentioned a few times throughout the canon,[15] yet this is not because Israel consistently observed the practice faithfully. Israel had gone wrong in their tithing both before the exile (Amos 4:4) and after the exile (Mal 3), but for quite different reasons:

> "Enter Bethel and transgress;
> In Gilgal multiply transgression!
> Bring your sacrifices every morning,

12. Mayes, *Deuteronomy*, 244.

13. Cairns, *Deuteronomy*, 221.

14. Christensen, *Deuteronomy 1:1—21:9*, 305.

15. Gen 14:28; Lev 27; Num 18; Deut 12; 14; 26; Amos 4:4; 2 Chron 31; Neh 10; 12; 13; Mal 3; Luke 11; 18; Heb 7.

Your tithes every three days.
"Offer a thank offering also from that which is leavened,
And proclaim freewill offerings, make them known.
For so you love to do, you sons of Israel,"
Declares the Lord God. (Amos 4:4–5)

In this passage God is parodying the Israelite priest in his call to worship; directing them with cultic instructions.[16] Ironically their commands go beyond requiring a tithe every third year to every third day, nevertheless they are still not fulfilling the law. The reason behind this judgment is that people are giving for wrong and selfish reasons; people were giving in order to enhance their own reputations.[17] Even still the poor were still being oppressed and God's justice was not being practiced, due to a corrupt priesthood.[18] It should not be missed that this passage demonstrates that the purpose of tithing is not merely to resource the income of the priests; ultimately it has to do with establishing God's justice.

Turning to the book of Malachi, quite different reasons are seen to be behind God's judgment of the priesthood.

> "Will a man rob God? Yet you are robbing me! But you say, 'How have we robbed You?' In tithes and offerings. You are cursed with a curse, for you are robbing me, the whole nation of you! Bring the whole tithe into the storehouse, so that there may be food in my house, and test me now in this," says the Lord of hosts, "if I will not open for you the windows of heaven and pour out for you a blessing until it overflows. Then I will rebuke the devourer for you, so that it will not destroy the fruits of the ground; nor will your vine in the field cast its grapes," says the Lord of hosts. "All the nations will call you blessed, for you shall be a delightful land," says the Lord of hosts. (Mal 3:8–12)

With the echo of Genesis 12:3 in Malachi 3:12, Malachi's words draw a direct correlation between Israel's practice of tithing

16. Stuart, *Hosea–Jonah*, 337.

17. Limburg, *Hosea–Micah*, 102.

18. Andersen, *Amos*, 434.

and God's mission to the nations. The so called "gifts" which are being offered to God, were completely worthless; they could not be eaten or even given away let alone sold.[19] Coming at a time when the land had suffered drought, crop failure, locust plague and blight, Malachi is challenging the privileged priesthood with regard to the abuse of their position in not distributing provision to those in need. Again it can be observed that the purpose of the tithe was not solely to resource the priesthood, for it also had a social dimension in that it provided for those who had no other form of support. By supporting the most vulnerable in their midst, Israelite society would look markedly different to the societies around them, standing as a testament of God's love.

The Israel of Amos and the Israel of Malachi had both in their own way misunderstood the place of tithing. Nevertheless God's purpose for the tithe and the measure by which he judged the Levites, remained the same. In both cases the priest's greed in putting himself above others and the very lack of concern for those who were marginalized, brought forth God's judgment. This though can be contrasted with what is found in Nehemiah, where tithing was done correctly; partly because the tithe was given in the right spirit (Neh 12:44), and partly because it allowed the Levites to fulfill the law and give themselves to service.[20]

In some ways, the paying of tithes ensured the nation's spiritual wellbeing. When the priesthood was not adequately maintained, the priests and the Levites were compelled to support themselves by other means. This inevitably meant that the worship of God and the teaching of his word were neglected. This is

---

19. Achtemeier, *Nahum–Malachi*, 179.

20. The idea that in the postexilic period there was a power struggle within the priesthood, and conflict over the tithing system (Holmgren, *Israel Alive Again*, 152) is completely false. If anything the context of Nehemiah implies the complete opposite, for whereas in the time of Moses there had been more Levites than priests, in the time of Nehemiah, there were more priests than Levites. Yet the priesthood did not alter the Scriptures to establish their own authority (Kaufmann, *Religion of Israel*, 193). Consequently there is no reason to think that the priesthood was solely seeking to substantiate their claim and edit the torah to their advantage.

noticeable in the story of Hezekiah. King Hezekiah determined to restore the temple worship of his day by reinstituting the tithing system and thereby underwriting the ministry of the priests and the worship of the Lord. Yet it should be noted that in Chronicles, it was not the Levites' responsibility to encourage people to give, that was the role of political authorities. The same can be seen in the book of Nehemiah, where civil leaders are given the blame for letting tithing slip.[21] Perhaps the point to draw from this is that the priesthood were not to regulate or force people to give.

To bring this conversation back to the metaphorical designation of the Levites as firstfruits, the Levites were to locate Israel's giving within God's heart for justice. As the model gift, the Levites were to ensure that alternative motives for giving did not usurp God's missional heart for justice which revealed God's nature to the surrounding nations. Clearly though this could not be achieved if the Levites refused to bear the humility required of them.

As it was in Amos, tithing is not just the act of giving; it is giving from a position of humility. The envisaged community was not one which was divided according to wealth.[22] Inevitably there would be groups and individuals who were not able to support themselves, such as the orphan and the widow. For these groups, the law made provision, enabling them to participate fully in God's blessing. Through their landlessness the priesthood would identify with these groups, for the giving would come from a position of fellowship, not superiority:

> At the end of every third year you shall bring out all the tithe of your produce in that year, and shall deposit it in your town. The Levite, because he has no portion or inheritance among you, and the alien, the orphan and the widow who are in your town, shall come and eat and be satisfied, in order that the Lord your God may bless you in all the work of your hand which you do. (Deut 14:28–29)

21. Allen and Laniak, *Ezra, Nehemiah, Esther*, 163.
22. Craigie, *Deuteronomy*, 234.

The Levites were to be a model for giving, demonstrating to the Israelites that giving should be done from the position of dependence upon God, not arrogance; just as God gave both the law and himself from a place of relational vulnerability, not of remote disinterest. In addition to the metaphor proclaiming the Levites to be firstfruits, the priesthood's landlessness is key to this understanding of humility, as will be seen in the following chapter.

The Levites as an enslaved people, the firstborn of Israel, reminded the nation that they were God's treasured possession. They belonged to him for he brought them out from Egypt, from the hand of Pharaoh. To be sure, the metaphor of slavery is not the only one used for the relationship between God and his people, for they are simultaneously a redeemed people. The enslavement of the priests then, reminded the people that they were all equal in the sight of God, in that everyone was dependent upon God's mercy and grace. This being the case, the Levites slavery demonstrated the attitude of servitude necessary for participating in God's mission.

7

The Priesthood as a Landless People

THE LAST CHAPTER PUT forward the idea that their designation as "firstfruits" enabled the Levites to administer God's justice. This idea will be further developed in this chapter in examining the Levites' landlessness.

The fact that the priests could not own land directly challenges the hypothesis that the priesthood constituted a dominant social and political class, in Israelite society. Von Rad openly admitted that the reasons behind this sociological phenomenon of priestly landlessness are "no longer clear,"[1] but suggested that historically the country priests had lost their livelihood through a process of centralization.[2] Others like Habel supposed that the priests could progressively acquire more and more land on a permanent basis, from those dedicated to the Lord.[3] By this interpretation, the Levites' landlessness was in fact a privileged position. Yet Leviticus 27 makes it clear that the consecration of land to the Lord still came under the Jubilee regulations. In these discussions, it is sometimes

1. Rad, *Deuteronomy*, 112.
2. Ibid., 103.
3. Habel, *Land Is Mine*, 112.

observed that priests could purchase land, as was the case in Jeremiah 32:7. However this was a separate case, because for Jeremiah this happened under the laws of redemption, and was a prophetic act, whereby this small piece of property is paradigmatic of the whole land.[4] More to the point, Jeremiah explicitly criticizes the priests for seeking to line their own pockets (6:13; 8:10), and declared that God will redistribute the land.

This chapter will begin by focusing on the sociological implications of the priesthood's landlessness, looking at the relationship between them and other landless groups within Israel and also the social function of the Levitical cities. The latter part of this chapter will then weigh the theological implications of their landlessness through rereading the stories at the end of Judges and considering the significance of the Lord being their inheritance.

THE LAND

In order to understand the missiological implications of the Levites' landlessness, Israel's land theology must first be appreciated. The story from Exodus to Deuteronomy is one of a journey from slavery to liberation, and from landlessness to a covenanted relationship with God, marked by land.[5] Coming from a context of slavery, the hope of God's theocratic and liberating rule was typified by the gift of land. For when the community lived within the boundaries of the covenant they would enjoy the blessings of the land, whereas neglecting the covenant would ultimately lead to exile (Deut 28). Yet even within this vision of covenanted land, there would inevitably be exceptions; the poor (Exod 23:6; Deut 15:7–11), the stranger (Exod 21:21–24; 23:9), the sojourner (Deut 10:19), the widow, orphan (Deut 24:19–22), and the Levite (Deut 14:27), all lived without land and so without power or dignity.

At this point a note of caution should be sounded: that the priesthood did not inherit any land does not mean they lived in

4. Thompson, *Book of Jeremiah*, 588.

5. Brueggemann, *Land*, 52.

a constant state of hopelessness. They were not solely meant to be landless, powerless and undignified as a mark of their dependence on God; to an extent they were also to be prosperous in dependence, to signify God's overwhelming love and provision for the whole community, which of course included the most vulnerable.[6] Nor should it be supposed that the landlessness of the Levites, or even that of other groups, excluded them from living in covenant with God, land in itself was only a symbol of a greater spiritual reality. The Levites lived in the midst of the tension which existed between the landed and the landless.[7] The relationship between these two groups was not to be one of exclusion, but the one which spoke of the love and fellowship they had in God. The Levites were to function as a gate, through which the powerless could pass, and thereby experience the blessings of being in relationship with God, even as the landed Israelites could. Through God's provision of the Levites, everyone could participate fully in the covenant and its promises.

THE LEVITICAL CITIES

The scattered dwelling of the Levites within the land, through the distribution of Levitical cities, was representative of God's presence in the midst of the nation, even as Israel was representative of God's presence in the midst of the nations that surrounded them. Being landless the Levites served to remind the Israelites, that ultimately they were not to be defined by the land itself but by the covenant which precluded it being given.

Though the Levites were not to own any land, Numbers 35 makes it clear that they were to be given some pastureland alongside the forty-eight cities. The small allotment of pastureland was necessary for gifts of livestock,[8] but the total area of the land given

---

6. McConville, *Deuteronomy*, 151.

7. Brueggemann, *Land*, 190.

8. Bellinger, *Leviticus and Numbers*, 314.

to them came to fifteen square miles, about 0.1% of the land.[9] This could have provided for some of their sustenance but certainly not all. In a context where land equated to wealth, the Levites were by no means self-sufficient, and even the land given to them was for dwelling not ownership.[10] The forty-eight cities, six of which were "cities of refuge" for the sake of administering justice, have been taken symbolically as four lots of twelve to the kingdom of God, were spread throughout the land.[11]

> Then the heads of households of the Levites approached Eleazar the priest, and Joshua the son of Nun, and the heads of households of the tribes of the sons of Israel. They spoke to them at Shiloh in the land of Canaan, saying, "The Lord commanded through Moses to give us cities to live in, with their pasture lands for our cattle." So the sons of Israel gave the Levites from their inheritance these cities with their pasture lands, according to the command of the Lord. (Josh 21:1–35)[12]

There is in the list of cities in Joshua 21 a hint of unreality for some of these cities, such as Gezer, had yet to be taken. Benjamin Mazar argued that the cities were those conquered by the Davidic monarchy where the Canaanite religion was firmly established, and the editor idealistically transposed these cities into the list in an attempt to hide their heritage.[13] According to this reading, the Levitical priesthood reinstitutionalized and rebranded the Canaanite religion. However this is to completely overlook the

9. Wenham, *Numbers*, 234.

10. Gottwald, *Tribes of Yahweh*, 696.

11. Keil and Delitzsch, *Commentary on the Old Testament*, 260.

12. Some such as Woudstra (*Book of Joshua*, 307) have motioned that these verses display an ill-disciplined observance to the stipulations given regarding the distribution of Levitical cities in Num 35:1–8; supposing that the cities were not distributed proportionately. Yet this simply is not correct, for Num 35 does not specify where or how many towns per tribe there should be (Hess, *Joshua*, 280). The point made by this passage is that the stipulations laid out in Num 35 are being observed and the deprived priesthood is being taken care of (Butler, *Joshua*, 232).

13. Mazar, "Cities of the Priests," 194.

differences between the Levitical priesthood and those of the surrounding nations. For example, it is known that the Hittite priesthood operated under the authority of the kings, who were also entitled to perform cultic rituals.[14] It is also known that the priestly establishments of the surrounding peoples consumed a high percentage of their nation's gross domestic product.[15] This is quite different from the Levitical priesthood which was not to be a wealthy elitist group, nor were they ultimately to come under the king's authority but under God's.

Mazar's hypothesis misses the point of the passage, for the list was composed in expectation of the conquest which would be made if they put their faith in what the Lord had promised in Joshua 13:6.[16]

The Levitical cities enabled the Levites to administer justice to the marginalized because they were situated throughout the land and enabled the Levites to exist as a supported landless group. This meant that the Levites were situated to serve and identify with all the Israelites including the landless.

THE LEVITES' INHERITANCE

The Levites did not receive a portion of the land as their inheritance, because the Lord was their inheritance, meaning that their communion with the Lord transcended even death.[17] Evidently the Levites' landlessness was the guarantee for the claim made by all Israelites that the Lord was their portion (Ps 16:5), and therefore the guarantee of their continuing occupation of the land. This

14. Taggar-Cohen, "Covenant Priesthood," 14.

15. Gottwald, *Tribes of Yahweh*, 614.

16. Woudstra, *Book of Joshua*, 310.

17. Goldingay supposes that this means that the Lord belongs to Levi (Goldingay, *Old Testament Theology*, 46). This though makes no obvious sense, for God could not be handed down as land could upon death (Habel, *Land Is Mine*, 34). Rather it makes more sense if the phrase is understood to mean that their communion could not be lost not even in the face of death (Rad, *Old Testament Theology*, 404).

hypothesis is shown to be true in examining the role of the Levites in the book of Judges.

Coming at the end of the book of Judges, two stories are told relating the accounts of two separate but similarly unnamed Levites. The anonymity of both the Levites permits the individual character to stand for the wider priesthood.[18] Of course, that these stories are recorded in the Bible does not mean that the Levites' actions have God's approval, nor does it mean that the Levites' knew no better. The passage's judgment would be unintelligible if the Levites' theological and social significance was only later worked out during the postexilic period. In the closing chapters of Judges, the narrator is detailing the extent of Israel's moral decline. These concluding episodes are intentionally painting Israelite religion at its worst; when the nation served false gods and the priesthood were too weak to do anything about it, thereby setting the stage for the story of Samuel.[19] The theological framework which unites the rest of Judges is suddenly broken. Whereas before there is a pattern that the people sinned, God handed them over to their enemies, the people cried out in distress to God and he raised up a deliverer; in these chapters God ceases to deliver his people, there is no cry for help and no judge.

The first of these two stories recorded in Judges 17–18, tells of a Levite who serves at the shrine of Micah, before stealing Micah's idol and joining the Danites in their conquest for land. In this story land is the major theme, as it records an unlicensed conquest which ensures the eventual destruction of Israel. The metal image taken from Micah ensnares the whole of the tribe of Dan in the sin of idolatry; idolatry which would later lead to the complete downfall of the north (2 Kgs 17:16). It is not just the Danites who are searching for land though, for their search is deliberately aligned with the Levite's own search for somewhere to live, and it is this which instigates the wider story.[20] In turning to the text itself, focus should be given to the following verses:

18. Younger, *Judges and Ruth*, 348.

19. Butler, *Judges*, 401.

20. Matthews, *Judges and Ruth*, 171. The Levite's wayward search for land

> Now there was a young man from Bethlehem in Judah, of the family of Judah, who was a Levite; and he was staying there. Then the man departed from the city, from Bethlehem in Judah, to stay wherever he might find a place; and as he made his journey, he came to the hill country of Ephraim to the house of Micah. Micah said to him, "Where do you come from?" And he said to him, "I am a Levite from Bethlehem in Judah, and I am going to stay wherever I may find a place." Micah then said to him, "Dwell with me and be a father and a priest to me, and I will give you ten pieces of silver a year, a suit of clothes, and your maintenance." So the Levite went in. The Levite agreed to live with the man, and the young man became to him like one of his sons. So Micah consecrated the Levite, and the young man became his priest and lived in the house of Micah. Then Micah said, "Now I know that the Lord will prosper me, seeing I have a Levite as priest." (Judg 17:7–13)

It was not unthinkable that a Levite could be a sojourner, indeed Deuteronomy 18:6–8 instructs such a Levite to move to the central sanctuary, for there he might expect to receive an equal portion. However, the Levite in our story goes wrong; his destination is not the central shrine, he does not join other Levites but replaces another unauthorized priest and he does not serve in the name of the Lord, but in the name of Micah.[21] The Levite puts himself up for sale to the highest bidder, and is happy to leave Micah when a better offer comes along, later in the story.[22] For Micah's part, his true motivation is prosperity (Judg 17:13), but his desire is for a prosperity without the corresponding demands on him for obedience.[23] His employment of the Levite is an attempt to manipulate the deity.[24] Yet Micah's opportunism which goes completely unchallenged is more than matched by the materialism

---

is therefore directly associated with the Assyrian conquest of 722 BCE.

21. Block, *Judges, Ruth*, 486.

22. Wilcock, *Message of Judges*, 159.

23. Hamlin, *Inheriting the Land*, 150.

24. Block, *Judges, Ruth*, 489.

of the Levite. The Levite's story goes from bad to worse, beginning in Bethlehem, a city which is not one of the forty-eight mentioned in Joshua 21, it is not long before he is practicing idolatry. He is a young Levite dissatisfied by his prospects in Bethlehem and it is his wayward search for prosperity which then leaves the Danites abandoned to their own wayward desire for land and prosperity.[25]

The Danites came to the Levite to enquire as to the Lord's will (Judg 18:5). This was quite unnecessary, as God had already revealed his will in the allotments of the land, and the land they sought to take did not belong to them, so there should have been no need for another enquiry. Dan's inheritance should have been in the southwest of Israel (Josh 19:40–46), but they had lost it to the Amorites (Judg 1:34). Despite this, the Levite duly tells the Danites to go in peace, assuring them of the Lord's favor; words which would provide the rationale for the slaughter of Laish, later in the chapter. This conquest though, certainly did not have the Lord's approval. The spies report that it is a land flowing with milk and honey, but say nothing of the people's wickedness; a fundamental reason which underpinned the giving of God's land to Israel in the first place (Deut 9:4–5).

This story demonstrates that when the Levites forsook their landlessness in search for prosperity, Israel's mission descended into tribal warfare, greed and idolatry. Just as the Levite's desire for land, prosperity and power eventually lead to the downfall of Israel, it also leads to a civil war against the tribe of Benjamin. The story that follows, the Levite and his concubine, is linked to the story of Micah by the common theme of the Levite's greed. This second story depicts the horrors of power and triumphalism alongside the abuse of a helpless woman;[26] where the Levite's heartless dismemberment of the concubine is emblematic of his treatment of Israel.[27]

In this story, the Levite is also said to be of the tribe of Judah, implying that he has disregarded his supra-tribal status, and

25. Boling, *Judges*, 255.
26. Trible, *Texts of Terror*, 65.
27. Klein, *Triumph of Irony*, 174.

reduced his Levitical status to a profession.[28] Not only does he desire prestige but he also desires to appear affluent; for he is able to afford a concubine presumably for the sole purpose of sexual gratification.[29] Undoubtedly though, his promiscuity also speaks of his unfaithfulness, and it becomes clear that the Levite's shameful conduct is situated at the very heart of Israel's rebellion.

The Levites' landlessness was to remind the whole of Israel that the Lord was their portion. This hope, that their covenant relationship with God would transcend even death, was the basis for their continued inhabitation of land and faithful participation within God's mission. When the Levites' abandoned this hope though, as was the case in the book of Judges, idolatry replaced a living relationship with the Lord and his mission became all but forgotten.

Building upon the link between justice and mission, this chapter saw that the Levites' landlessness placed them in a position to be able to offer God's provision and blessing to the other landless groups: the poor, the foreigner, the widow and the orphan.

---

28. Nelson, *Raising Up a Faithful Priest*, 4.
29. Butler, *Judges*, 417.

8

The Priesthood and the New Covenant

EARLIER IN THIS STUDY, it was noted when examining Zechariah 3 that the priesthood function symbolically, to demonstrate the holiness which would characterize the messianic rule. In this chapter, the role of the Levitical priesthood in the canon after Christ will be further explored, making particular reference to Hebrews 7, 1 Peter 2, and the book of Revelation.

God's covenant with the Levites is unbreakable and permanent, and is attested to be so at various moments throughout the canon (e.g., Exod 40:15; Num 25:13; Jer 33:17). In particular, Numbers 18:19 describes God's covenant with Levi as a "covenant of salt," that is, a covenant which is eternal and indissoluble.[1] The perpetual nature of God's covenant with the Levites provides an appropriate backdrop for the study of the Levitical priesthood in the "new covenant." So before turning to texts in the New Testament, it would seem appropriate to first consider the theology of Chronicles together with Jeremiah 33.

First and Second Chronicles were put together in the postexilic period, and is essentially a retelling of a large portion of

1. Davies, *Numbers*, 190.

Israelite history in the light of the prophetic tradition, where the hope which the postexilic community had for the future, shapes a retelling of the past. As a result, the Chronicler only tells the story of the line of David and pays particular interest to the Levitical priesthood and the ways in which their actions prefigure the actions of God through his anointed one. So for example, in the light of God's promise to David, the chronicler idealizes the reign of Solomon, not because he wants his audience to forget Solomon's shortcomings but to point forward to the rule of the coming son of David. Solomon is commended for establishing orderly worship; through providing for the Levites and building the temple, which has the purpose of bringing all peoples to worship the Lord.

This close alignment between God's promises to David and his covenant with Levi, stem from Jeremiah 33.

> For thus says the Lord, "David shall never lack a man to sit on the throne of the house of Israel; and the Levitical priests shall never lack a man before Me to offer burnt offerings, to burn grain offerings and to prepare sacrifices continually." The word of the Lord came to Jeremiah, saying, "Thus says the Lord, 'If you can break my covenant for the day and my covenant for the night, so that day and night will not be at their appointed time, then my covenant may also be broken with David my servant so that he will not have a son to reign on his throne, and with the Levitical priests, my ministers. As the host of heaven cannot be counted and the sand of the sea cannot be measured, so I will multiply the descendants of David my servant and the Levites who minister to me.'" (Jer 33:17–22)

It is in the face of societal disintegration and the destruction of the temple, that Jeremiah's words are spoken; assuring Israel that God had not completely forsaken his people, nor stripped its leadership of their role. If ever there was an opportunity for God to rid himself of his covenant commitments, it was the exile. Yet it is precisely at that moment that God promised a renewal of his covenant with them (Jer 32:40).

It should be noted that within the wider context of Jeremiah 33:14–26, God's faithfulness to the covenants with David and Levi are secured by his covenant with creation and his promise to Abraham. God's covenant with the day and the night; his covenant with the world he created, is the guarantee that he will never break his covenant, neither with David nor with the Levites. The line of David and the Levitical priesthood, share in the same promise.[2] Consequently it would be impossible to affirm God's commitment to provide a Messiah from the line of David, and yet at the same time suggest that his commitment to the Levites had been brought to an end. Despite this, a significant portion of New Testament theologians do just that; maintaining that the Levitical priesthood had been "superseded"[3] by Christ's and as a result had been brought to an end.[4]

To be facile by way of introduction, thinking on the subject of Israel's relationship to the church might well be split into two categories. Some have sought to show that Israel's story continues after Christ and runs parallel to the story of the church. Others have argued that the story of Israel has been replaced by a greater narrative, that of the church.[5] This chapter on the Levitical priesthood in the New Testament, attempts to take the continuity of God's covenant with Israel as seriously as the first category, while also being as committed to the notion of God's solitary mission and purpose, contained within the second. Specifically then, it will be argued here that God's covenant with Levi is continued in Christ, and only in Christ.

2. Thompson, *Book of Jeremiah*, 602.

3. Morris, *New Testament Theology*, 308

4. Ellingworth, *Epistle to the Hebrews*, 370.

5. For more detailed outlines of the two respective views, consult Russell and Cohn's *Dual-Covenant Theology* and Soulen's *God of Israel and Christian Theology*.

THE BOOK OF HEBREWS

Pivotal to any understanding of the role of the Levites in light of Christ, is one's interpretation of Hebrews. The point being made in this section, is not that the book of Hebrews makes the same arguments as have been made throughout this study, but that it is not theologically inconsistent with them. Hebrews 7 perhaps provides a difficult challenge to the hypothesis that there is a coherent theology of the Levites which transcends the canon, so it is important to evaluate this text closely.

> Now if perfection was through the Levitical priesthood (for on the basis of it the people received the Law), what further need was there for another priest to arise according to the order of Melchizedek, and not be designated according to the order of Aaron? . . . Jesus has become the guarantee of a better covenant. The former priests, on the one hand, existed in greater numbers because they were prevented by death from continuing, but Jesus, on the other hand, because he continues forever, holds his priesthood permanently. Therefore he is able also to save forever those who draw near to God through him, since he always lives to make intercession for them. For it was fitting for us to have such a high priest, holy, innocent, undefiled, separated from sinners and exalted above the heavens; who does not need daily, like those high priests, to offer up sacrifices, first for his own sins and then for the sins of the people, because this he did once for all when he offered up himself. (Heb 7:11, 22–27)

In order to fully grasp the implications of this passage, it is important to first of all consider the context into which Hebrews was written. Hebrews is not a divine textbook meant to answer all questions regarding the relationship between the various covenants. Rather it needs to be appreciated that Hebrews is a written address and an example of "epideictic rhetoric"; written to encourage its hearers to take a different course of action.[6] It is widely thought that the letter's Jewish audience was tempted in the

---

6. Witherington, *Letters and Homilies*, 49.

face of persecution to abandon the teaching of Christ, returning to their previous practice of faith.[7] For this reason, the writer begins by employing a practice known, in ancient forms of rhetoric, as *synkrisis*; a process of comparing and contrasting two alternative actions, beginning with the least controversial arguments in order to gain a hearing.[8] By Hebrews 7, the writer has reached one of the more contentious issues, and the now familiar execution of *synkrisis* is again put to use, comparing the old and new priesthoods on a number of points before climaxing with a resounding note of praise for Jesus' "better covenant" (Heb 7:22). However, the writer of Hebrews does not seek to belittle this other covenant; *synkrisis* compares two subjects of similar quality, to demonstrate the eminence of the one.[9] The writer does not contrast the good with the bad, but the good with great. Therefore the argument being put forward seeks to assert the brilliant stature of Jesus' priesthood, not primarily the pointlessness of the Levitical system.

It cannot then be said that the Levitical priesthood had been "replaced"[10] nor that it had "failed"[11] as many commentators attempt to do.[12] Yet some go even further still, to suggest that the Levitical system was "designed to fail,"[13] being decreed by God from the very beginning.[14] Needless to say, no such decree exists. This commonly held view fails to take seriously enough the perpetual nature of God's covenant with Levi, nor does it appreciate the writer's rhetorical strategy outlined above. Essentially, either there is no theology of the Levitical priesthood which transcends

7. Bearing in mind that it was probably written before the destruction of the temple in 70 CE

8. Witherington, *Letters and Homilies*, 232.

9. Allen, *Hebrews*, 408.

10. Stedman, *Hebrews*, 82.

11. Schmitt, "Restructuring Views on Law," 198.

12. Hebrews does talk of the "first covenant" having fault and being made "obsolete" by the "new covenant" (Heb 8:13), but it does so within the eschatological framework of the "now and not yet."

13. Koester, *Hebrews*, 359.

14. Bruce, *Epistle to the Hebrews*, 166.

the canon, or the nuanced argument found in Hebrews needs to be explained for what it is, a nuanced argument to a particular audience.

Approaching the text of Hebrews through a sociological lens, Richard Johnson attempted to critique the role of the Levites by implementing Mary Douglas's "Grid and Group" model.[15] Johnson argued that first-century CE Hellenistic Judaism was a "strong group, strong grid," or hierarchist society.[16] In contrast the writer of Hebrews envisions a "low grid" society, evidenced in the kinship between the Son and the believers, and the absence of an elevated leadership.[17] Johnson struggles however to determine whether the envisaged community is a "strong group"; on the one hand it has a clear group identity which transcends time to include all the people of God, yet on the other hand there is a disregard for identity boundaries typical in "weak group" societies.[18] This is clearly then of the type of enclavist society envisaged by the book of Numbers, which demonstrate a similar disregard to "boundaries."[19] If Johnson's assessment is accepted then the writer of Hebrews is not being critical of the ideological Israel, but of the particular Jewish social framework found in the first century CE. This would be entirely consistent with Jesus' criticisms of the Levites and indeed that of Old Testament prophets, observed earlier in this study.

In addition to the language of "failure" and "replacement," it is often said that Christ "fulfilled" the Levitical priesthood. The usage of this term is quite obscure, as it seems to be used by all parties and burdened with a wide variety of meanings. Some speak of fulfillment in the sense that it had been brought to an end,[20] while others speak of fulfillment as the effectuation of the old Levitical system which was insufficient in and of itself. Though this latter view pays recognition to the relationship between the two priestly

15. Johnson, *Going Outside the Camp.*

16. Ibid., 66.

17. Ibid., 97.

18. Johnson, *Going Outside the Camp*, 97.

19. Douglas, *In the Wilderness*, 49.

20. Joslin, *Hebrews, Christ and the Law*, 168.

orders, it still misses the mark. The ministry of the Levitical priesthood was effective, when administered faithfully, and is said to be so throughout the Hebrew canon.[21] Christ's priesthood is the richest and purest enactment of that faithfulness, and so it becomes impossible to hold to the one without the other. To underscore this point Hebrews 7 must be examined closely to see how and in what ways the Christ's priesthood is "better."

Hebrews 7 presents two different kinds of priestly orders, Levi's and Melchezidek's. The question that must be asked of the passage is how and to what extent they are different? Frank Thielman contends that there are two differences; first he says that Jesus' priesthood is different because it was perfected through suffering, and second because unlike the sacrifices of the Levites, Jesus' sacrifice was fully effective for salvation.[22] In responding to his first point, this study has sought to show that the Levites were to suffer hardship and without doing so it was impossible for them to fulfill their role faithfully. As for Thielman's second argument, there is nothing to suggest that the sacrifices of the Levites were by their very nature ineffective, except when they were offered in a spirit different from that exhibited by Christ.

The main difference expressed in Hebrews 7, is that Jesus' priesthood is a Messianic or royal priesthood. Melchezidek is the only other person who functions both as a king and a priest, and he upholds the Levitical order because he came before it.[23] The story of Melchezidek therefore does not undermine the Levitical priesthood but supports it,[24] and it is impossible, on this basis, to argue that Christ's priesthood then "supersedes" that of the Levites.[25] Christ's priesthood is different because he could

---

21. The point here is not that the Levitical system did not need Christ or point to him, but rather to accommodate the wider witness of Scripture into an interpretation of Hebrews. Clearly those worshipping before Christ did experience salvation in a real way (e.g., Ps 51:11–12), yet Christ is the fullest expression of their faith and hope.

22. Thielman, *Theology of the New Testament*, 602.

23. Jorgensen, "Hebrews 7:23–28," 297.

24. Johnson, *Hebrews*, 181.

25. Songer, "Superior Priesthood," 355.

also function as a king, and his kingship was different because he could function as priest, as no other king was permitted to do. The passage also makes it clear that, Christ's priesthood is different because it is eternal, but it cannot be said from the text that it is different in essence.

The theology of the Levitical priesthood having already been put forward in this study, allows for observations concerning the similarities between the two priesthoods to be made. Jesus taught selflessly (Luke 4:43), offered himself as a sacrifice (Matt 20:28), acted as a servant to others (John 13) and was landless (Matt 8:20); all for the sake of God's mission, setting a precedent for the people of God and for the sake of inviting others to participate in God's kingdom rule.

1 PETER 2

If God's covenant with Levi is continued in the person of Christ; then surely the relationship between Jesus and the people of God, should be seen to emulate that held by the Levites and the ancient Israelites. This is evident, both in 1 Peter (1 Pet 2:5, 9) and the Apocalypse of John (Rev 1:6; 5:10; 20:6), which both draw upon the language of Exodus 19:6, to expound the community's relationship to Jesus the high priest. This can be observed in the vision of Jesus as the high priest in Revelation 1:13 which follows the declaration that God has made his people to be a kingdom of priests (Rev 1:6). First Peter also affirms this relationship:

> And coming to him as to a living stone which has been rejected by men, but is choice and precious in the sight of God, you also, as living stones, are being built up as a spiritual house for a holy priesthood, to offer up spiritual sacrifices acceptable to God through Jesus Christ . . . But you are a chosen race, a royal priesthood, a holy nation, a people for God's own possession, so that you may proclaim the excellencies of him who has called you out of darkness into his marvelous light; for you once were not

> a people, but now you are the people of God; you had not
> received mercy, but now you have received mercy.
>
> Beloved, I urge you as aliens and strangers to abstain
> from fleshly lusts which wage war against the soul. Keep
> your behavior excellent among the Gentiles, so that in
> the thing in which they slander you as evildoers, they
> may because of your good deeds, as they observe them,
> glorify God in the day of visitation. (1 Pet 2:4–5, 9–12)

The recipients of Peter's letter were experiencing various
kinds of trials and varying degrees of persecution, so Peter writes
primarily to reassure and comfort them through their trials.[26] The
letter's purpose is outlined in 1 Peter 1:13, a verse which shapes
the discourse, and urges them to be holy even as God is holy (Lev
19:2).[27] The following pericope (1 Pet 1:13–2:10), which has just
been cited, is an expansion on what it means for Peter's audience
to be a holy people.[28]

John Elliott suggests that the word "priesthood" is really
just another way of saying "holy and elect."[29] This though seems
unlikely, for it would be strange for Peter to use a metaphor and
expect his audience to rid it of its natural connotations.[30] Nor is
it likely that Peter insinuates that his audience constitute a "new
spiritual priesthood," as has also been suggested,[31] for nowhere
does Peter address his readers as a distinctly "new" community.[32]
Such a reading goes directly against Peter's purposes to encourage his readers by pointing to God's faithfulness throughout their
shared history with the people of God in the Old Testament.

Rather this priesthood who are under the high priest of Jesus,
have all the hallmarks of the Levitical priesthood. They are to have
a ministry of proclamation, teaching both the people of God and

---

26. Jobes, *1 Peter*, 42.

27. Witherington, *Letters and Homilies*, 93.

28. Schreiner, *1, 2 Peter, Jude*, 47.

29. Elliott, *Elect and the Holy*, 185.

30. Kelly, *Commentary on the Epistles of Peter and Jude*, 93.

31. Grudem, *First Epistle of Peter*, 111.

32. Michaels, *1 Peter*, 107.

the Gentiles about God's greatness (1 Pet 2:9), they are landless (1 Pet 2:11) at least until the day of visitation. They are as slaves ransomed by Christ (1 Pet 1:18) and they are to be holy, offering sacrifices through Jesus Christ (1 Pet 2:5).[33]

BAPTISM AND PRIESTLY CONSECRATION

There are two good reasons for affirming the connection between baptism and priesthood. The first reason, is that of all the ritual washings in the Old Testament, only three were to be administered by another; cleansing from leprosy (Lev 14:1–7), cleansing after touching a corpse (Num 19:1–22) and priestly consecration (Exod 29:1–9). While of course the rite of baptism cannot be limited to any one of these, they provide a good theological backdrop for understanding the rite. Possibly this is true also of John's baptism; where John functioned to consecrate a priestly people, albeit that this is not explicitly stated in the gospels.

The second reason can be found in Hebrews 10:

> Therefore, brethren, since we have confidence to enter the holy place by the blood of Jesus, by a new and living way which He inaugurated for us through the veil, that is, His flesh, and since we have a great priest over the house of God, let us draw near with a sincere heart in full assurance of faith, having our hearts sprinkled clean from an evil conscience and our bodies washed with pure water. (Heb 10:19–22)

As only priests could enter the holy place the passage makes clear that Jesus sanctifies believers and brings them into the priesthood. he does this through sprinkling them with his blood and washing them with pure water (Heb 10:22), a likely reference to baptism.[34]

---

33. The metaphor of sacrifice is also used elsewhere in the New Testament (Rom 12:1; Heb 13:15–16), to refer to the practice of offering praise, doing good works, and offering oneself.

34. O'Brien, *Letter to the Hebrews*, 367.

While not wanting to limit the meaning of baptism, one connotation it likely carried was that of being consecrated into the priesthood. This is further evidence that God's intentions for Israel and Levi are continued in Christ, who consecrates believers and makes them into a priestly nation.

THE TWENTY-FOUR ELDERS

To close this chapter, it is worth briefly considering the image of the twenty-four elders who gather to worship around the throne in the book of Revelation (4:4, 10; 5:8; 11:16; 19:4). The primary role of these twenty-four elders is to worship the one seated on the throne, although Revelation 5:8 also gives them the responsibility of bringing the prayers of the saints before the lamb.

The symbolic value of the twenty-four is recognized in light of 1 Chronicles 24, where David organizes the Levitical priesthood into twenty-four divisions. As is often the case in the postexilic canonical literature, Chronicles places great virtue on the King's treatment of the priesthood; when the priesthood are being supported, the king or governor is seen to be honoring God. David's ordering of the Levitical priesthood is therefore seen positively by the chronicler.

Given both the function of the elders in Revelation, in worshipping and presenting the prayers before the throne, and the relationship between the temple and the throne of God, it seems that the twenty-four elders are best taken as a reference to the twenty-four divisions of the priesthood.[35] If this is indeed true, then the New Testament ends with a vision referencing God's faithfulness to the covenants with both David and Levi, woven together in the majesty of the lamb seated on the throne.

The twenty-four elders being representative of God's people in heaven, illustrates that the priestly mission of God's people has

35. The identity of the twenty-four elders has been widely discussed; others have argued that they represent the twelve patriarchs and the twelve apostles, a separate angelic order and the counterpart of the Babylonian pantheon of God's (Mounce, *Book of Revelation*, 126).

not been discarded. While the shape of the Levitical priesthood continually changed, God's intention for it remained and has been brought to its fullest expression in Christ.

This chapter has argued that the Levites' mission is incorporated in the priesthood of Christ; affirming God's faithfulness to his covenant with Levi. Christ does not just take on the hallmarks of the Levitical priesthood, he also insists that God's people serve under his priesthood, in order for them to participate in his mission.

Unfortunately all too often the Scripture's message emanating from the Levitical priesthood has been silenced. Resemblances of supersessionism in the book of Hebrews, have been allowed to limit and deprive God's people from meditating on their priestly identity. The Levites have been treated like distant cousins, bearing an inkling of likeness to the modern church leader. Yet the Old Testament's presentation of the ideological priesthood has the power to inform, shape and even transform contemporary thinking on the role of leadership and the mission of his priestly people.

9

Conclusion

THIS STUDY HAS TRIED to show the legitimacy of reading the theology of the Levitical priesthood as a coherent whole, evident throughout the canon. If the hypothesis is to be accepted then there are certain implications which must be thought through. In closing, the implications that the study has for biblical theology and for the church will be considered, respectively. Within these two sections the specific foci of humility and mission, which have underscored the study, will be attended to.

IMPLICATIONS FOR BIBLICAL THEOLOGY

The reconstructions of Israelite history, which centered on the cult, have had enormous repercussions for Old Testament theology. If indeed there is one coherent theology of the Levitical priesthood, albeit expressed differently at different times of Israelite history, then it means there is more continuity in thought between the sources and the final composition of the texts than source criticism has typically allowed for. In addition, if this coherence is true of the cult, then it would follow that it must be true also for the wider theology of the Old Testament, because the cult lie at the heart of Israel's worship and theological reflection.

The idea that the priesthood were a political power adapting sources for their own benefit and convenience, should also affect the way theologians interact with the Bible today. It should surely give good precedent for similarly handling biblical texts. Conversely if the Levitical ministry was to be rooted in humility and reverence for God's word then a faithful reading of the text must also be undertaken in the same manner. Though it is sometimes argued otherwise; a canonical reading of Scripture is fundamentally at odds with source critical approaches which have their roots in reconstructed histories.

What are the implications for biblical theology, if the priesthood's missional nature is accepted? Is a missional reading of the text simply another contextual hermeneutic or is it *the* proper way to read and interpret the text? Can a canonical study of the priesthood exist, which does not speak of their missional role?

It has been argued throughout, that the concept of mission is found in the text. Key to this hypothesis has been a specific interpretation of Exodus 19:6; yet additional evidence has been observed throughout, to corroborate this interpretation. Special mention should be made of the chapter on "Priesthood and Worship" which demonstrated that the Levitical priesthood inform the missional theology shared by the nation.

The most significant implication arising from the fact that it is the text which has a concern for mission, and not just the reader, is that it affirms the relationship between theology and the church. If the Bible itself has a central concern for mission, then all biblical theology should maintain such a focus. Theology should therefore serve to resource, empower and equip missional communities to faithfully administer their missional role to those around them.

This being the case it is fitting to close by also considering the implications that this study has for the church.

IMPLICATIONS FOR THE CHURCH

The theology emanating from the Levitical priesthood should be a great source of encouragement and guidance for Christians and leaders in particular, as they seek to live missionally within their own contexts. In thinking through the implications for the church, the Western context in particular will be reflected upon, but of course the scope of application is wider reaching.

Church communities must together seek to reflect the God they serve, and the leadership has a key role within this. This study has sought to emphasize the fact that mission is first and foremost something which God is doing. Within this though, mission is something that the whole community is involved in and participates in. The role of a leader is fundamentally to assist God's people in participating in God's mission. This mission is holistic in its witness; touching upon areas of faithful administration of justice, teaching which is grounded in God's word and corporate representation of God and his character. God's people must be equipped and empowered in all of these areas, and the leader plays a key function in all three.

In thinking through just some particular implications for the way the church thinks about mission, space will be given specifically to the themes of "church structure", "blessing" and "worship."

Church Structure

Leaders of God's people today must also give attention to the structure of their communities and consider its part in the community's witness. Does the local church within an individualist society still maintain their enclavist shape? It is easy to forsake the ideological structure, whether it is in the name of "contextualization" or through not realizing its importance in directing the community's spirituality and witness. Yet in a post-Christendom context as well, where people sometimes have more issue with the church than with the gospel, this question should not be overlooked and it is worth considering whether the role of a church's structure has allowed people to misconstrue the gospel.

Though church polity is often considered a secondary issue, it directly informs the witness of the community. Is a God of justice being framed by the communal experience of a God of grace? Or perhaps for some churches the opposite is the problem; a God of justice is in reality downplayed, because there is little or no hierarchical leadership.

One key aspect in shaping such a community identified in the course of this study, is to live within the metaphor of the leadership being a gift and sacrificial offering on behalf of the people. Life within this metaphor does not only affect the way a community views their leaders but also affects the way that communities train and raise up future leaders.

Blessing

In some traditions a church service will always end with a "blessing." This practice correctly understood has the power to shape and empower missional communities. Blessing should affirm the missional identity of the congregation, not the exclusive status of the person blessing or be merely an exclamation of good will. This is a key function for the church leader and equips the congregation to realize their missional role in the world.

Worship

It is difficult to make generalizations about worship in the church today, but at least questions can be asked: do leaders truly appreciate the pedagogical role of worship? Do training institutions encourage leaders to place such value on worship? Do the songs which are sung accommodate a holistic theology which shape missional communities?

Worship is the direct responsibility of leaders, who have a duty to facilitate worship both in spirit and in truth.

How might humility be defined, given the theology of the Levitical priesthood? First, it should be emphasized that the Levites did not just take on a lowly position, they took on a lowly position in relation to others and in relation to God. It is easy to be led astray on this point; humility is not simply self-humiliation or self-deprivation. Rather humility is a relational positioning in order to serve. The Levites are a clear embodiment of this point. They were to make themselves low in order that they might serve even the lowest in their community and reveal truth to them. To go to one extreme, is to abase oneself so much that meaningful service is no longer an option. This is in fact a fake imitation of humility and manifests itself as self-righteousness and pride dressed up as humility.

Humility is also taking a correct position before God. It is a selflessness which strives toward holiness and a confidence rooted in his generosity. With regards this later point; the Levites functioned within the knowledge that the Lord was their inheritance and he would watch over them and provide for them. Moreover they were to function from a position of authority, but an authority which had been given to them in order they also might empower others.

In weighing up more specifically the implications of the Levites for how the church thinks about humility, the themes of "devotion" and "service" will be highlighted.

Devotion

For an environment which idolizes family, in the void of meaning and societal disintegration, the leaders of God's people today must clearly point to the fact that devotion of the Lord must come first. While it is often not helpful to dualize between faithfulness to the family and faithfulness to the Lord, the testimony of God's interaction with the Levites demonstrates that God demands devotion to his word and mission above and beyond "faithfulness" to the family.

Another question to ask is whether the metaphor of slavery is being lived out today, or whether Christians restrict themselves to the metaphor of redemption? God has taken his people out from the authority of the world and has taken them to be his own slaves. His people are both slaves working for his glory and renown and simultaneously a redeemed people. Perhaps it is too easy for contemporary readers to hear the words "treasured possession" and not think about being enslaved to God; living for him as his "possession." This identity gives clear ethical demands about living lives in humility before God. To help God's people realize their identity, God requires leaders to work within the metaphor of being enslaved to him; being devoted entirely and solely to him.

Service

In a climate where religion and forms of spirituality are marketed to fit the needs and desires of individuals, the gospel cannot be compromised in following the example of hollow and deceptive philosophies. Comfort cannot replace costly devotion: this requires both correct presentation of the message and leaders whose lives reflect this. Teaching from a position of humility and recognizing the cost of discipleship, is essential to this task of not compromising the gospel.

In addition to this, it might also be observed that humility facilitates godly giving, and for this purpose the church and her leaders must take a lowly position. Just as God gives from a position of relational humility, so must the church offer the gospel to the world in like manner.

Does the church today give from a position of relational humility? Do leaders tangibly live to identify themselves with the marginalized in society? In order to make their witness sincere and godly, God's gifts should not be administered from a position of superiority but one of relationship rooted in humility. This directly challenges cultural understandings of compassion, which can be reduced to feelings of pity and the outworking of guilt.

The leader should be landless. Even if the example of earthly leaders, the "priests" of the surrounding nations are most certainly "landed," it is all the more reason for leaders of God's people to be "landless." This is testament both to the congregation and to the world of God's own graciousness and love.

Bibliography

Achtemeier, Elizabeth. *Nahum–Malachi*. Atlanta: John Knox, 1986.

Allen, David. *Hebrews*. Nashville: Broadman & Holman, 2010.

Allen, Leslie. *Ezekiel 20–48*. Dallas: Word, 1990.

Allen, Leslie, and Timothy Laniak. *Ezra, Nehemiah, Esther: Based on the New International Version*. Peabody, MA: Hendrickson, 2003.

Andersen, Francis, et al. *Amos: A New Translation with Introduction and Commentary*. York: Doubleday, 1997.

Ashby, Godfrey. *Go Out and Meet God: A Commentary on the Book of Exodus*. Grand Rapids: Eerdmans, 1998.

Ashley, Timothy. *The Book of Numbers*. Grand Rapids: Eerdmans, 1993.

Barton, John, and John Bowden. *The Original Story: God, Israel and the World*. London: Darton, Longman & Todd, 2004.

———. *Reading the Old Testament: Method in Biblical Interpretation*. London: Darton, Longman & Todd, 1996.

Bauckham, Richard, et al. *Bible and Mission: Christian Witness in a Postmodern World*. Carlisle, UK: Paternoster, 2003.

Beeby, Dan. *Canon and Mission*. Harrisburg, PA: Trinity International, 1999.

Bellinger, William. *Leviticus and Numbers: Based On The New International Version*. Peabody, MA: Hendrickson, 2001.

Blackburn, Ross. *The God Who Makes Himself Known: The Missionary Heart of the Book of Exodus*. Downers Grove: InterVarsity, 2012.

Blauw, Johannes, and Victor Hayward. *The Missionary Nature of the Church: A Survey of the Biblical Theology of Mission*. London: Lutterworth, 1962.

Blenkinsopp, Joseph. *Gibeon and Israel: The Role of Gibeon and the Gibeonites in the Political and Religious History of Early Israel*. Cambridge: Cambridge University Press, 1972.

Block, Daniel. *The Book of Ezekiel: Chapters 25–48*. Grand Rapids: Eerdmans, 1998.

———. *Judges, Ruth*. Nashville: Broadman & Holman, 1999.

Boling, Robert. *Judges: Introduction, Translation and Commentary*. Garden City: Doubleday, 1975.

Bibliography

Brown, Raymond. *The Message of Numbers: Journey to the Promised Land.* Nottingham, UK: InterVarsity, 2002.

Bruce, Frederick. *The Epistle to the Hebrews.* Grand Rapids: Eerdmans, 1990.

Brueggemann, Walter. *First and Second Samuel.* Louisville: John Knox, 1990.

———. *The Land: Place as Gift, Promise, and Challenge in Biblical Faith.* London: SPCK, 1978.

———. "Theodicy in a Social Dimension." In *Social-Scientific Old Testament Criticism: A Sheffield Reader,* edited by David Chalcraft, 260–80. Sheffield, UK: Sheffield Academic, 1997.

———. *Theology of the Old Testament: Testimony, Dispute, Advocacy.* Minneapolis: Fortress, 1997.

Budd, Philip J. *Leviticus.* New Century Bible Commentary. London: Pickering, 1996.

Butler, Trent. *Joshua.* Word Biblical Commentary. Waco, TX: Word, 1983.

———. *Judges.* Word Biblical Commentary. Nashville: Nelson, 2010.

Cairns, Ian. *Deuteronomy: Word and Presence.* Edinburgh: Handsel, 1996.

Childs, Brevard. *Old Testament Theology in a Canonical Context.* Minneapolis: Fortress, 1986.

Chirichigno, Gregory. *Debt Slavery in Israel and the Ancient Near East.* Sheffield, UK: JSOT Press, 1993.

Christensen, Duane. *Deuteronomy 1:1—21:9.* Word Biblical Commentary. Nashville: Nelson, 2001.

Coggins, Richard. *Introducing the Old Testament.* Oxford: Oxford University Press, 1990.

Cole, R. Dennis. *Numbers.* New American Commentary. Nashville: Broadman & Holman, 2001.

Cooper, Lamar E. *Ezekiel.* New American Commentary. Nashville: Broadman & Holman, 1994.

Craigie, Peter C. *Deuteronomy.* New International Commentary on the Old Testament. Grand Rapids: Eerdmans, 1976.

Creach, Jerome. "The Psalms and the Cult." Chapter 6 of *Interpreting the Psalms: Issues and Approaches,* edited by David Firth and Peter Johnston. Nottingham, UK: InterVarsity, 2005.

Cross, Frank. *Canaanite Myth and Hebrew Epic: Essays in the History of Religion of Israel.* Cambridge: Harvard University Press, 1997.

Curtiss, Samuel I. *The Levitical Priests: A Contribution to the Criticism of the Pentateuch.* Charleston, SC: BiblioBazaar, 2009.

Davies, Eryl. *Numbers.* New Century Bible Commentary. London: Marshall Pickering, 1995.

Demarest, Gary. *Leviticus.* Communicator's Commentary. Dallas: Word, 1990.

Douglas, Mary. "The Background of the Grid Dimension: A Comment." *Sociological Analysis* 50 (1989) 171–76.

———. *In the Wilderness: The Doctrine of Defilement in the Book of Numbers.* Sheffield, UK: Sheffield Academic, 1993.

———. *Leviticus as Literature.* Oxford: Oxford University Press, 2001.

————. *Natural Symbols: Explorations in Cosmology*. London: Barrie & Jenkins, 1973.

Driver, Samuel. *Notes on the Hebrew Text of the Books of Samuel*. Charleston, SC: BiblioBazaar, 2009.

Duguid, Iain. *Ezekiel*. NIV Application Commentary. Grand Rapids: Zondervan, 1999.

Duke, Rodney. "Punishment or Restoration? Another Look at the Levites of Ezekiel 44:6–16." *JSOT* 40 (1988) 61–81.

Durham, John I. *Exodus*. Word Biblical Commentary. Waco, TX: Word, 1987.

Durkheim, Emile, and Joseph Swain. *The Elementary Forms of the Religious Life: The Classic Sociological Study of Primitive Religion*. New York: Collier, 1961.

Ellingworth, Paul. *The Epistle to the Hebrews: A Commentary on the Greek Text*. Carlisle, UK: Paternoster, 1993.

Elliott, John. *The Elect and the Holy: An Exegetical Examination of 1 Peter 2:4–10 and the Phrase "Basileion Hierateuma."* Leiden: Brill, 1966.

Evans, Mary. *The Message of Samuel: Personalities, Potential, Politics and Power*. Nottingham, UK: InterVarsity, 2004.

Firth, David G. *1 & 2 Samuel*. Apollos Old Testament Commentary. Nottingham, UK: Apollos, 2009.

Fishbane, Michael. "1 Samuel 3: Historical Narrative and Narrative Poetics." In *Literary Interpretations of Biblical Narratives*, edited by R. Kenneth et al., 2:191–203. Nashville: Abingdon, 1982.

Fretheim, Terence E. *Exodus*. Interpretation series. Louisville: John Knox,1991.

Goheen, Michael. *A Light to the Nations: The Missional Church and the Biblical Story*. Grand Rapids: Baker Academic, 2011.

Goldingay, John. *Old Testament Theology*. Vol. 2, *Israel's Faith*. Milton Keynes, UK: Paternoster, 2006.

Gottwald, Norman. *The Hebrew Bible: A Socio-Literary Introduction*. Philadelphia: Fortress, 1985.

————. *The Tribes of Yahweh: A Sociology of the Religion of Liberated Israel, 1250–1050 BCE*. Sheffield, UK: Sheffield Academic, 1999.

Gross, Jonathan. *Measuring Culture*. New York: Columbia University Press, 1985.

Grudem, Wayne. *The First Epistle of Peter: An Introduction and Commentary*. Leicester: InterVarsity, 1988.

Gunneweg, Antonius. *Understanding the Old Testament*. Translated by John Bowden. London: SCM Press, 1978.

Habel, Norman. *The Land Is Mine: Six Biblical Land Ideologies*. Minneapolis: Fortress, 1995.

Hamlin, John. *Inheriting the Land: A Commentary on the Book of Joshua*. Edinburgh: Handsel, 1983.

Harrison, Roland. *Leviticus: An Introduction and Commentary*. Leicester: InterVarsity, 1980.

Hartley, John. *Leviticus*. Word Biblical Commentary. Dallas: Word, 1992.

Hempel, Johannes. *Die Israelischen Ansauusnen von Segen und Fluch im Lichte altorientalischer parallelen*. Leipzig: Brockhaus, 1925.

Hess, Richard. *Joshua: An Introduction and Commentary*. Leicester: InterVarsity, 1996.

Holmgren, Fredrick. *Israel Alive Again: A Commentary on the Books of Ezra and Nehemiah*. Edinburgh: Handsel, 1987.

Houtman, Cornelis. *Exodus*. Vol. 2. Historical Commentary on the Old Testament. Kampen: Kok, 1996.

Hyatt, James. *A Commentary on Exodus*. London: Oliphants, 1971.

Isenberg, Sheldon, and Dennis Owen. "Bodies, Natural and Contrived: The Work of Mary Douglas." *Religious Studies Review* 3 (1977) 1–17.

Jobes, Karen H. *1 Peter*. Baker Exegetical Commentary on the New Testament. Grand Rapids: Baker, 2005.

Johnson, Luke Timothy. *Hebrews: A Commentary*. New Testament Library. Louisville: Westminster John Knox, 2006.

Johnson, Richard W. *Going Outside the Camp: The Sociological Function of the Levitical Critique in the Epistle to the Hebrews*. Sheffield, UK: JSOT Press, 2002.

Jorgensen, Janyce. "Hebrews 7:23–28." *Interpretation* 57 (2003) 297–99.

Joslin, Barry. *Hebrews, Christ and the Law in Hebrews 7:1—10:18*. Eugene, OR: Wipf & Stock, 2009.

Kaiser, Walter. *Mission in the Old Testament: Israel as a Light to the Nations*. Grand Rapids: Baker, 2000.

Kane, J. Herbert. *Christian Missions in Biblical Perspective*. Grand Rapids: Baker, 1976.

Kaufman, Stephen. "A Reconstruction of the Social Welfare Systems of Ancient Israel." In *In the Shelter of Elyon: Essays on Ancient Palestinian Life and Literature*, edited by J. Spencer et al., 277–86. Sheffield, UK: JSOT Press, 1984.

Kaufmann, Yechezkel. *The Religion of Israel: From Its Beginnings to the Babylonian Exile*. Chicago: University of Chicago Press, 1960.

Keil, Carl, and Franz Delitzsch. *Commentary on the Old Testament in Ten Volumes*. Vol. 1, *The Pentateuch*. Grand Rapids: Eerdmans, 1973.

Kelly, John. *A Commentary on the Epistles of Peter and of Jude*. London: Black, 1969.

Kidner, Derek. *Ezra and Nehemiah: An Introduction and Commentary*. Leicester: InterVarsity, 1979.

Kiuchi, Nobuyoshi. *Leviticus*. Apollos Old Testament Commentary. Nottingham, UK: Apollos, 2007.

Klein, Lillian. *The Triumph of Irony in the Book of Judges*. Sheffield, UK: Almond Press, 1988.

Koester, Craig. *Hebrews: A New Translation with Introduction and Commentary*. London: Yale University Press, 2001.

Langston, Scott. *Exodus Through the Centuries*. Boston: Wiley Blackwell, 2005.

Lapham, Henry. *The Bible as Missionary Handbook*. Cambridge: Heffer, 1925.

Lefebvre, Michael. "Torah Meditation and the *Psalms*: The Invitation of *Psalm 1*." In *Interpreting the Psalms: Issues and Approaches*, edited by Firth, D. et al., 213–25, Nottingham, UK: Apollos, 2005.

Levenson, Jon. *The Death and Resurrection of the Beloved Son: The Transformation of Child Sacrifice in Judaism and Christianity*. London: Yale University Press, 1995.

Levine, Baruch A. *Leviticus*. Philadelphia: Jewish Publication Society, 1994.

———. *Numbers 1–20*. London: Yale University Press, 2007.

Limburg, James. *Hosea–Micah*. Atlanta: John Knox, 1988.

Martin-Achard, Robert. *A Light to the Nations: A Study of the Old Testament Conception of Israel's Mission to the World*. London: Oliver & Boyd, 1962.

Matthews, Victor H. *Judges and Ruth*. New Cambridge Bible Commentary. Cambridge: Cambridge University Press, 2004.

Mayes, Andrew. *Deuteronomy*. New Century Bible Commentary. Grand Rapids: Eerdmans, 1981.

Mazar, Benjamin. "The Cities of the Priests and the Levites." *Vetus Testamentum Supplements* 7 (1959) 193–205.

McConville, J. G. *Deuteronomy*. Apollos Old Testament Commentary. Leicester: Apollos, 2002.

———. *The Law and Theology in Deuteronomy*. Sheffield, UK: Continuum International, 1987.

McNeile, Alan. *The Book of Exodus: With Introduction and Notes*. Charleston, SC: BiblioBazaar, 2010.

Mendelsohn, Isaac. *Slavery in the Ancient Near East: A Comparative Study of Slavery in Babylonia, Assyria, Syria and Palestine from the Middle of the Third Millennium to the End of the First Millennium*. Westport, CT: Greenwood, 1978.

Merrill, Eugene. *Haggai, Zechariah, Malachi: An Exegetical Commentary*. Richardson: Biblical Studies, 2003.

Michaels, Ramsey. *1 Peter*. Word Biblical Commentary. Waco, TX: Word, 1988.

Milgrom, Jacob. *The Encroacher and the Levite: The Term Aboda*. Studies in Levitical Terminology. Berkeley: University of California Press, 1970.

———. *Leviticus: A Continental Commentary*. Minneapolis: Augsburg Fortress, 2004.

———. *Leviticus 1–16*. Anchor Bible Commentaries. New Haven: Yale University Press, 2007.

Miller, Patrick. *The Religion of Ancient Israel*. Louisville: Westminster John Knox, 1987.

Morris, Leon. *New Testament Theology*. Grand Rapids: Zondervan, 1986.

Motyer, Alec. *The Prophecy of Isaiah*. Leicester: InterVarsity, 1993.

Mounce, Robert. *The Book of Revelation*. Grand Rapids: Eerdmans, 1998.

Mowinckel, Sigmund. *Segen und Fluch in Israels Kult und Psalmendichtung*. Kristiana: Videnskapsselskapets Skrifter I, Histo.-Filos, 1923.

Nelson, Richard. *Raising Up a Faithful Priest: Community and Priesthood in Biblical Theology*. Louisville: Westminster John Knox, 1993.

Bibliography

O'Brien, Peter. *The Letter to the Hebrews*. Grand Rapids: Eerdmans, 2010.

Okoye, James. *Israel and the Nations: A Missionary Theology of the Old Testament*. Maryknoll: Orbis, 2006.

Oswalt, John. *The Book of Isaiah: Chapters 40–66*. Grand Rapids: Eerdmans, 1998.

Pedersen, Johannes. *Israel: Its Life and Culture*. London: Oxford University Press, 1926.

Peters, George. *A Biblical Theology of Missions*. Chicago: Moody Press, 1972.

Rad, Gerhard von. *Deuteronomy: A Commentary*. London: SCM Press, 1996.

———. *Old Testament Theology*. Vol. 1, *The Theology of Israel's Historical Traditions*. Translated by David Stalker. Edinburgh: Oliver & Boyd, 1962.

Ramirez, Guillermo. "The Social Location of the Prophet Amos." In *Prophets and Paradigms: Essays in Honor of Gene M. Tucker*, edited by S. Reid, 112–24. Sheffield, UK: Sheffield Academic, 1996.

Rodd, Cyril. "On Applying a Sociological Theory to Biblical Studies." In *Social-Scientific Old Testament Criticism: A Sheffield Reader*, edited by D. Chalcraft, 22–33. Sheffield, UK: Sheffield Academic, 1997.

Routledge, Robin. *Old Testament Theology: A Thematic Approach*. Downers Grove: InterVarsity, 2008.

Rowley, Harold. *The Missionary Message of the Old Testament*. London: Carey, 1944.

Russell, Jesse, and Ronald Cohn. *Dual-Covenant Theology*. London: Bookvika, 2012.

Schmitt, Mary. "Restructuring Views on Law in Hebrews 7:12." *Journal of Biblical Literature* 128 (2009) 189–201.

Schreiner, Thomas. *1, 2 Peter, Jude*. New American Commentary. Nashville: Broadman & Holman, 2003.

Smith, Gary. *Hosea, Amos, Micah*. NIV Application Commentary. Grand Rapids: Zondervan, 2001.

Songer, Harold. "A Superior Priesthood: Hebrews 4:14—7:28." *Review and Expositor* 82 (1985) 345–59.

Soulen, Kendall. *The God of Israel and Christian Theology*. Minneapolis: Augsburg Fortress, 1996.

Stedman, Ray. *Hebrews*. IVP New Testament Commentary. Leicester: InterVarsity, 1992.

Steinfels, Peter. "The Myth of Primitive Religion." *Commonweal*, October 1970, 495–501.

Stuart, Douglas K. *Exodus*. New American Commentary. Nashville: Broadman & Holman, 2006.

———. *Hosea-Jonah*. Word Biblical Commentary. Waco, TX: Word, 1987.

Taggar-Cohen, Ada. "Covenant *Priesthood*: Cross-Cultural Legal and Religious Aspects of Biblical and Hittite *Priesthood*." In *Levites and Priests in Biblical History and Tradition*, edited by M. Leuchter et al., 11–24. Atlanta: SBL, 2011.

Thielman, Frank. *Theology of the New Testament: A Canonical and Synthetic Approach*. Grand Rapids: Zondervan, 2005.

Thompson, J. A. *The Book of Jeremiah.* New International Commentary on the Old Testament. Grand Rapids: Eerdmans, 1980.

———. *1, 2 Chronicles.* New American Commentary. Nashville: Broadman & Holman, 1994.

Tidball, Derek. *The Message of Leviticus: Free to be Holy.* Downers Grove: InterVarsity, 2005.

Tiemeyer, Lena. *Priestly Rites and Prophetic Rage.* Tubingen: Mohr Siebeck, 2006.

Trible, Phyllis. *Texts of Terror: Literary-Feminist Readings of Biblical Narratives.* London: SCM Press, 1984.

VanGemeren, Willem. *New International Dictionary of Old Testament Theology and Exegesis.* Vol. 4. Carlisle: Paternoster, 1997.

Wellhausen, Julius. *Prolegomena to the History of Ancient Israel.* Edinburgh: Black, 1885.

Wells, Jo. *God's Holy People.* JSOTSup 305. Sheffield, UK: Sheffield Academic, 2000.

Wenham, Gordon J. *The Book of Leviticus.* New International Commentary on the Old Testament. Grand Rapids: Eerdmans, 1979.

———. *Numbers.* Old Testament Guides. Sheffield, UK: Sheffield Academic, 1997.

———. *Psalms as Torah: Reading Biblical Song Ethically.* Grand Rapids: Baker Academic, 2012.

Wevers, John. *Ezekiel.* New Century Bible Commentary. Grand Rapids: Eerdmans, 1982.

White, Leland. "Grid and Group in Matthew's Community: The Righteousness/ Honor Code in the Sermon on the Mount." *Semeia* 35 (1986) 61–90.

Wilcock, Michael. *The Message of Judges: Grace Abounding.* Leicester: InterVarsity, 1992.

Williamson, Hugh. *Ezra, Nehemiah.* Word Biblical Commentary. Waco, TX: Word, 1985.

Witherington, Ben. *Letters and Homilies for Hellenized Christians.* Vol. 2, *A Socio-Rhetorical Commentary on 1–2 Peter.* Downers Grove: InterVarsity, 2007.

———. *Letters and Homilies to Jewish Christians.* Leicester: Apollos, 2008.

Woudstra, Marten. *The Book of Joshua.* New International Commentary on the Old Testament. Grand Rapids: Eerdmans, 1981.

Wright, Christopher. *The Mission of God: Unlocking the Bible's Grand Narrative.* Downers Grove: InterVarsity.

———. "'Prophet to the Nations': Missional Reflections on the Book of Jeremiah." In *A God of Faithfulness,* edited by J. Grant et al., 112–29. Edinburgh: T. & T. Clark, 2011.

Wright, Christopher Mitchell. *The Meaning of BRK "To Bless" in the Old Testament.* SBL dissertation series. Atlanta: SBL, 1987.

Younger, K. Lawson. *Judges and Ruth.* NIV Application Commentary. Grand Rapids: Zondervan, 2002.

Made in the USA
Coppell, TX
26 June 2024

33941932R00066